Wild Nevada

To Julie Gomez
Keep it wild!
Roberta Moore
September 8, 2020

Wild Nevada

TESTIMONIES ON BEHALF OF THE DESERT

Edited by

Roberta Moore and Scott Slovic

Foreword by Michael Frome

University of Nevada Press
Reno & Las Vegas

University of Nevada Press, Reno, Nevada 89557 USA
www.unpress.nevada.edu
Copyright © 2005 by University of Nevada Press
All rights reserved
Manufactured in the United States of America
Design by Omega Clay

Library of Congress Cataloging-in-Publication Data
Wild Nevada : testimonies on behalf of the desert / edited by Roberta Moore and
Scott Slovic ; foreword by Michael Frome.—1st ed.

p. cm.

ISBN 978-0-87417-613-1 (pbk. : alk. paper)
1. Wilderness areas—Nevada. 2. Wilderness areas in literature. 3. Nevada—
Description and travel. 4. Desert ecology—Nevada. I. Moore, Roberta, 1949–
II. Slovic, Scott, 1960– III. Title.
F845.W55 2005
979.3'03—dc22 2004020180

The paper used in this book meets the requirements of American National Standard for
Information Sciences—Permanence of Paper for Printed Library Materials,
ANSI/NISO Z39.48-1992 (R2002). Binding materials were selected for
strength and durability.

Credits: "Finding the Space in the Heart," from The Gary Snyder Reader by Gary
Snyder. © 1999 by Gary Snyder. Reprinted by permission of Counterpoint Press, a
member of Perseus Books, L.L.C.; "Nevada," from Blood Sister, I Am To These Fields
by Linda Hussa, used by permission of Black Rock Press, University of Nevada,
Reno; "I Kneel to See the Dead Great Horned Owl" from 10 Moons and 13 Horses by
Gary Short, used by permission of University of Nevada Press; "The Future of the
Great Basin" by Michael Cohen, © 1997 by Michael Cohen, used with permission
from Chronicle Books, L.L.C.; "Nevada No Longer," from Bathing in the River of
Ashes by Shaun T. Griffin, used by permission of University of Nevada Press;
"Nevada Wilderness: What Good Is It?" from The Big Outside by Dave Foreman
and Howie Wolke, copyright © 1992 by Dave Foreman, used by permission of Harmony
Books, a division of Random House, Inc.

This book is dedicated to Nevada's wild country. The editors will donate all royalties
from the sale of this volume to Friends of Nevada Wilderness, an organization
devoted to educating the public about the grandeur, resources, and vulnerability of
Nevada's wilderness.

This book has been reproduced as a digital reprint.

CONTENTS

Foreword

MICHAEL FROME

In the process of reviewing the written materials that make up this book, I found myself absorbed in discovering a part of America that I had never known before. I followed the words and the pages leading me through a large, wild, and wonderful outback rising up from broad dunes and desert to peaks above 10,000 feet. I made my reading journey in the company of guides who know their terrain intimately, care about it, and want us all to understand it better. In prose and poetry, thirty writers, assembled here by Roberta Moore and Scott Slovic for the Friends of Nevada Wilderness, give their eloquent testimonies for a Nevada beyond the cities, casinos, suburban malls and sprawls.

They show clearly that "Nevada is not a wasteland," to be debased with the storage of toxic nuclear waste or by other mistakes of contemporary civilized society. To the contrary, they describe the colors and aromas and ancient history that endure in sandstone walls, limestone cliffs, and high mountain passes. And they want these special places to be recognized and protected as part of the National Wilderness Preservation System, which Congress established with passage of the Wilderness Act of 1964.

Their commitment is understandable, considering that creative persons have forever sought the primeval as source material and inspiration. Literature, poetry, and science, as Ralph Waldo Emerson wrote, all are homage to the unfathomed secrets of nature. Ansel Adams, the celebrated photographer, explained it this way: "Here are worlds of experience beyond the world of aggressive man, beyond history, beyond science. The moods and qualities of nature and the relations of great art are difficult to define; we can grasp them only in the depths of our perceptive spirit."

The testimonies reveal wilderness as a spiritual, or religious, treasure. One quoted Isaiah, my favorite Old Testament prophet. Another offered a prayer for Nevada's wild places. That makes sense to me. More than a century ago John Muir wrote that he was uplifted and exalted in the sanctuary of the wild. Wilderness to him was an expression of God on Earth—the mountains, God's temples; the forests, sacred groves. To Muir I will add that in a sacred place all life is sacred, and the humblest are holy and blessed.

Wilderness is the sacred place for renewal and healing, where "education" and "recreation" take on different meaning. A psychologist might prescribe a wilderness experience because of its freedom from evidences of critical or harmful human actions, or to find release from stress through stillness and solitude in the primeval. There are no social values to conform to; it is classless—all parties become essentially equal, benefiting from cooperation rather than competition. The individual acquires a sense of scale, conceding there is something larger and longer-lasting than anything he or she has known before and feeling that he or she belongs at the bosom of a much greater whole—and at peace.

The work of Friends of Nevada Wilderness depends upon the efforts of citizen volunteers cooperating with resource professionals. Together they have carefully profiled each of Nevada's Wilderness Study Areas and found them worthy of inclusion in the National Wilderness Preservation System. This leads me to note that citizen responsibility has always been the vital measure of difference. Virtually every tract of land worth saving that we now take for granted has been set aside because people cared—individuals who organized groups and then campaigned through the political process, without regard for personal reward.

As a case in point, William Gladstone Steel, from the first time he saw Crater Lake in 1885, worked tirelessly, building support and scientific data and influencing Oregon's congressional delegation until the national park was established in 1902. Later he said: "Aside from the United States government itself, every penny that was ever spent in the creation of Crater Lake National Park came out of my pocket and, besides that, it required many years of hard labor that was freely given. . . . All the money I have is in the park, and if I had more it would go there too." In contrast to other great American lakes, such as Tahoe, that fall in the category of paradise lost, Crater Lake, thanks to Steel, retains much of its natural character, a priceless shred of the original America.

I look back to the 1950s, when the proposed construction of dams in Dinosaur National Monument, Utah, though remote and little known, was defeated by a nationwide citizen campaign. Without broad citizen involvement in the 1960s and 1970s, there would be no national parks in the redwoods of California or within the North Cascades of Washington State or on the frontiers of Alaska. Were it not for caring citizens, the Colorado River would be dammed where it runs through the Grand Canyon, and the great forests would be long gone from the Olympic Peninsula.

Deep personal revelations that open the heart to feeling and open the mind to articulate compassion are the root of wilderness preservation. Howard Zahniser, the principal advocate of the Wilderness Act of 1964, was studious, articulate, and compassionate. "We are not fighting progress," Zahniser said. "We are making it. We are not dealing with a vanishing wilderness. We are working for a wilderness forever."

In 1956 Representative John P. Saylor of Pennsylvania introduced the Wilderness Bill in the House of Representatives. For eight years Saylor led the uphill legislative battle and never gave up. In 1961, when the going was tough, he declared: "I cannot believe the American people have become so crass, so dollar-minded, so exploitation-conscious that they must develop every last little bit of wilderness that still exists." Saylor's faith in Americans was sustained when Congress passed the Wilderness Act in 1964. The act has since proven its value many times over. The wilderness system has grown to encompass more than 107 million acres all across America, from Alaska to Puerto Rico, administered by four federal agencies: Bureau of Land Management, Fish and Wildlife Service, Forest Service, and National Park Service.

Theodore Roosevelt once said, "Aggressive fighting for the right is the noblest sport the world affords." Activism on behalf of wilderness is a thoroughly patriotic response worthy of Roosevelt's challenge. A wholesome natural environment provides the foundation for a wholesome human environment. We can't have one without the other. To consciously advance respect for living nature is to advance the national welfare and human dignity.

I believe that wilderness is the heart of the American ideal, that those choice fragments of Earth still wild, mysterious, and primeval nourish the soul and spirit of the nation and all its people. That we, with respect and reverence, have set aside these special places is known throughout the world; wilderness preservation as part of our way of life makes a far better and more welcome calling card to other nations than all the armed might we can muster.

The preservation of wild, unmanipulated nature is a use in its own right—a "wise use." Theodore Roosevelt made this clear early in the last century. "There is nothing more practical than the preservation of beauty," he said in talking of the big trees of California, "than the preservation of anything that appeals to the higher emotions of mankind." Gifford Pinchot, Roosevelt's close advisor and the pioneer of forestry in America, said it this way: "The vast possibilities of our great future will become realities only if we make ourselves, in a sense, responsible for that future. The planned and orderly development and conservation of our natural resources is the first duty of the United States. It is the only form of insurance that will certainly protect us against the disasters that lack of foresight has in the past repeatedly brought down on nations since passed away."

A nation deprived of liberty may win it, a nation divided may reunite, but a nation whose natural resources are destroyed must inevitably pay the penalty of poverty, degradation, and decay.

Wilderness is our great reservoir of hope—of salvation and redemption—to place it on the spiritual and moral plane. Billions of dollars have been drained out of the public till for military actions, as if we could democratize the world through force. But saving the wilderness, along with the effort to extricate America from global misadventures, marks a true test of democratic principles. The most important legacy our generation can leave is not a world at war. We must face the twenty-first century with new emphasis on human care and concern, including a point of view embodied in the protection of wild places that no longer can protect themselves.

The pope, when he visited the United States a few years ago, declared: "We need more than social reformers; we need saints." I would say, "We need more than social reformers; we need revolutionaries—not to commit violent deeds, but to press society to reorder its priorities, with emphasis on stewardship of God's green earth." The testimonies in this book remind me again and again that saving wilderness in Nevada preserves origins and diversity, for desert bighorn sheep, cougar, golden eagle, turkey vulture, red-tailed hawk, horned lizard, cutthroat trout and pupfish, and by so doing preserves origins, diversity, and destiny for humankind.

Wild Nevada

Introduction

SCOTT SLOVIC AND
ROBERTA MOORE

Mention the phrase "Nevada wilderness" to people outside of the state a few decades ago, and they would likely assume you meant the rough-and-tumble frontier sensibility in mining towns like Virginia City, the wild nightlife of the Las Vegas Strip, or perhaps the concussive intensity of nuclear explosions at the Nevada Test Site. The notion that Nevada, the nation's thirty-sixth state, established in 1864 during the Civil War, is also an extraordinarily beautiful place, intrinsically rich in both natural *wonders* and natural *resources,* has evolved more slowly. The seventh-largest state with 110,561 square miles of land, Nevada in 2002 had a human population of 2,173,491—this makes it fortieth in population out of the fifty states. Despite their relatively small numbers, Nevadans, since the arrival of Europeans, have worked the land rather heavily, particularly by way of large and small mining operations, sheep and cattle grazing, water use for urban communities and arid-land farming, some logging, and of course the testing of military ordnance, both nuclear and "conventional." The rapid growth of Nevada's major urban centers, Reno in the north and Henderson and Las Vegas in the south, will accentuate the pressure on land and water resources in this region. It is important that we find ways of promoting discussion of what kind of world we wish to inhabit in the future, what kind of place we hope to leave behind for our children and their children.

In the spirit of sustaining earlier discussions and prompting new conversations about Nevada's future, and about the future of public lands throughout the American West, we have undertaken this project. This particular volume was inspired by several other wilderness testimony projects that have been published in recent years. In 1995, Stephen Trimble and Terry Tempest Williams quickly rounded up a collection of statements in support of wilderness preservation in southern Utah and distributed a limited edition of that book to members of the United States Senate and House of Representatives. Another edition of that anthology, titled simply *Testimony: Writers of the West Speak on Behalf of Utah Wilderness,* appeared the following year from Minneapolis publisher Milkweed Editions. In 2001, Hank Lentfer and Carolyn Servid published *Arctic Refuge: A Circle of Testimony,* a volume of statements against drilling for oil in Alaska's Arctic National Wildlife Refuge, also with Milkweed Editions. Other testimony projects devoted to the preservation of specific wild places, such as Verne Huser's *Voices from a Sacred Place: In Defense of Petroglyph National Monument* (self-published in 1998), have appeared in the meantime.

Wild Nevada includes statements by some of the leading politicians, literary artists and scholars, and environmental and community activists from within Nevada's borders and from nearby states. Contributors range from ranchers and rangers to academics and government officials. Despite the eclectic backgrounds of the writers, and despite their varied perspectives on public policy, they are united in their devotion to the ecological and aesthetic values of this vast region of mountains and desert.

The thirty individual testimonies collected here were solicited as personal statements—the precise viewpoints and topics were not dictated to the authors. Therefore, what we have gathered is a varied, sometimes even contradictory, assemblage of perspectives. This is entirely appropriate for a state that prides itself as a haven for free thinking and individuality, for urban revelry and utter wilderness solitude, and sometimes even for social experiments in wild places, such as the annual Burning Man event in the Black Rock Desert. We offer these lively and diverse statements as a way of discerning how contemporary citizens of the American West feel about the idea of wilderness in one of the wildest regions in the lower forty-eight states.

Several of the essays that follow contribute subtle observations to the political and philosophical discussions of wilderness that heat up the halls of academia and public policy these days, but most of these statements do not pretend to change the way we think about the concept of wilderness. Theirs is actually the humbler aim of offering personal testimony about a place in the world that has often been misunderstood. With the recent designation of 451,915 acres of wilderness in Clark County in the southern part of the state, Nevada now has approximately two million acres of designated wilderness within its borders. Presently, United States Senators Harry Reid and John Ensign and Representative Jim Gibbons are working on the Eastern Nevada Public Lands Bill which will, if passed, designate new wilderness areas in Lincoln and White Pine Counties. This particular book, in itself, may not contribute directly to the formation of public policy in the way that Utah's *Testimony* contributed to the Clinton Administration's decision to create Grand Staircase–Escalante National Monument in 1996, but *Wild Nevada* is powerful evidence that Nevadans and other westerners are thoughtfully attuned to the current discussions about whether or not to create more official wilderness area in this state that consists of well over 80 percent federal land.

Many of the testimonies collected here consist first and foremost of stories of personal encounters with wild places in Nevada. Colorado author Ann Zwinger writes in her essay that "It's the particulars that tie me to the natural world. . . ." Such personal stories are rich with particulars of experience. Brian Beffort cautions us at the outset that Nevada is a "shy" place and we'll need patience and careful attention to get to know "her." The detailed observations offered in Peter Bradley's essay show exactly what it means to be attentive—to see beyond the apparent emptiness of this wide-open landscape. Linda Hussa's poem, with its refrain of "nothing . . . nothing . . . nothing," ironically depicts a landscape full of beautiful rock, animals, and light. Western Shoshone contributor Laura Rainey-Carpenter complicates the politics of wilderness protection by suggesting that official wilderness designation actually makes it harder for certain people, such as her elderly mother and young son, to experience the traditional lands of their people, while essayist Robert Leonard Reid argues that because "Americans, all of us, want and use too much," because of our lack of self-control and foresight, we need wilderness designation to protect what we love against ourselves. We love wild places not because they necessarily give us things we can immediately value and feel enriched by, but rather, as Robert McGinty says, because the land "sells nothing, makes no promises, promotes no cause." Some of us, such as activist Marge Sill, have recognized the importance of wild places for a long time. She offers stories from a half-century of loving—and fighting for—Nevada wilderness. Poet Gary Snyder sums up his own love for wild Nevada: "—the wideness, the / foolish loving spaces / full of heart."

While many of the pieces collected in this book present brief or extended narratives of personal experience, others emphasize broader historical, geographical, or philosophical contexts for the discussion of wilderness in Nevada. Cheryll Glotfelty, for instance, considers why wilderness is a relevant concept, an important kind of place, even in our era of global commerce and ever-present technology. "Wilderness areas will be where we go when we want to be offline," she says. Directing her gaze from older maps to more recent "Nevada Wilderness Status Maps," and also to the land itself, Ann Ronald emphasizes how the "status" of land changes over time, and she issues readers a challenge to "save" wild landscapes for future generations, "if we care, and if we dare." Jon Christensen wonders how we can compel ourselves to protect places that seem, at first glance, ugly and useless. He plays off of John Muir's nineteenth-century disparagement of the Nevada landscape, exploring the connections between landscape aesthetics and wilderness preservation. He helps us to understand how we might begin to appreciate what Snyder calls "the wideness, the foolish loving spaces." Michael P. Cohen, too, takes on the topic of accepting the reality of this place, explaining how people "begin to notice that [a particular place] is full of things that make it what it is." Stephen Trimble points out the illusion that there is little urgency in decisions to protect Nevada's wild places: Some argue that "because Nevada is so wild . . . we need not rush to designate wilderness." He cautions advocates not to be lulled into thinking the backcountry is "safe from destructive change." Lilace

Mellin Guignard shows specifically the kinds of destructive changes that might be forestalled through wilderness designation. Lest these contextualizing commentaries seem like mere intellectual speculation and poetic fancy, two of Nevada's United States senators, Richard Bryan (1988–2001) and Harry Reid (1986–), offer their own recollections of particular legislative efforts to protect land in this state that is, as Senator Reid puts it, "defined and blessed in part by what is not there." Michael Frome's learned foreword helps to place current discussions of Nevada wilderness into the larger context of the history of conservation politics in the United States.

Because of its perceived emptiness, including its relatively small population of voters, Nevada has long been on the list of most likely sites for conducting hazardous activities, such as weapons experimentation, and storing unwanted things, such as nuclear waste. During the height of the Cold War, the Nevada Test Site, located a hundred miles north of Las Vegas, was the site of nearly 1,000 nuclear explosions, both aboveground and below. In the 1970s, nuclear scientists and public officials began to think it might be necessary to find a centralized storage area for the dangerously radioactive by-products of America's nuclear power plants and nuclear weapons facilities. Currently, this nuclear waste is stored at 131 separate locations. Experts have estimated that spent fuel rods and liquid wastes, which continue to accumulate daily, would cover more than seventeen football fields if packed together in storage containers. After considering a variety of permanent nuclear repository sites throughout the American West, the U.S. Department of Energy determined in 2002 that Nevada's Yucca Mountain, located on the Test Site, would be the dump for all of the nation's high-level radioactive waste. This decision was made in defiance of public outcry, both within the state and beyond. The state's national representatives, Republicans and Democrats, are unified in their opposition to the Yucca Mountain repository, which is slated to begin receiving nuclear waste after 2010. Because use of the Nevada Test Site for weapons experimentation and nuclear waste storage is directly relevant to public lands issues in the state, several contributors to this book have touched upon or emphasized these issues. Rebecca Mills asks a series of questions that go right to the heart of the Yucca Mountain issue, including "When will we realize we should not produce something we do not know how to manage safely?" Shaun Griffin refers obliquely and hauntingly to Nevada's nuclear despoliation, alluding to the land's "loins of uranium down deep." For Scott Slovic, military reserves such as Yucca Mountain are an ironic extension of the "gated mountain" syndrome that has begun to plague the state's urban areas, where sprawling subdivisions increasingly block public access to beautiful wild places. Terry Tempest Williams, in her essay for this collection, argues that Nevada already has a "history of sacrifice in the name of war [and] should now be given her due for the high price paid in our nation's nuclear history." She argues that the Test Site should be designated a wilderness area as a "gesture of faith and forgiveness." Western Shoshone spiritual leader Corbin Harney warns that our activities at the Test Site are "making our Mother sick. . . . If you don't think about it," he cautions, "then the nature itself is going to make you think about it."

For many people beyond Nevada's borders, the state has become known as the nation's expendable desert location for military testing and the storage of horrible things. For others, Nevada is known for its cities—its opportunities for urban, indoor escape from ordinary life. Apart from their casino culture, their neon canyons, cities such as Las Vegas and Reno also offer remarkable opportunities for nearby wilderness experience. Within a few minutes' drive from downtown Reno, hikers make their way to a variety of striking landscapes, such as the Mt. Rose Wilderness Area. Corey Lee Lewis reminds us that nearby wilderness is not only a Reno phenomenon, but is also, for the time being, available even near metropolitan Las Vegas, in such places as Brownstone Basin. Patricia Swain, too, emphasizes the great value of having wilderness located so close to cities, celebrating "this state's riot of wealth" that includes trails not far from home.

Although Nevada may well be one of the most urban states in the nation (with most of its residents packed into the

Reno–Sparks–Carson City area in the north or Las Vegas–Henderson in the south), many residents live in remote, small towns or at least work in rather remote and wild locations. Several of the book's contributors live or work "on the land" as ranchers, scientists, or park rangers. Cattle rancher Brent Eldridge offers a perspective on wilderness protection that demonstrates the potential for "profit takers" and environmentalists to work together and achieve "reasonable protection of our wilderness resources." K. Alden Peterson, thinking like a scientist, traverses Nevada's mountain ranges and asks, "What would Nevada look like if all the humans believed resource use should stop well before animals, plants, mountains, and deserts began dying—before ecosystems collapsed?" And ranger Roberta Moore, from Great Basin National Park (the only national park in the state), considers the spiritual and psychological connections to wilderness that inspire her work and her life.

Many of the essays and poems collected in this book provide reasoned arguments for or against wilderness designation, but rational analyses and arguments are not the only focus of this collection. Perhaps the emotional core of this book—the emotional core of the debate about wilderness—occurs in the poetic evocations that appear throughout *Wild Nevada,* both in prose and in verse. "Is Nevada empty? Barren? Desolate?" asks activist Dave Foreman, and then he paints a prose poem of this place that resoundingly answers in the negative. Novelist Steven Nightingale, too, offers a lyrical meditation on the importance of wild places in his life, concluding, "In the Great Basin's bounty of light, anyone can learn what counts, what is useful." We have Shaun Griffin's cautionary poem about the irradiation of this mysterious, scarcely known place called Nevada, and Linda Hussa's meditation that depicts the rich emptiness of this place. When Gary Short poetically narrates the experience of witnessing owl feathers in a tree, telling us "The tree was filled with feathers of silver / that pulsed and thrilled," we retain some of that emotional energy the next time we walk through the woods, pulsing and thrilling to know that we exist in such a magical world.

This book began in the spring of 2002 when Roberta Moore, moved by her love of wild places and wild things and inspired by the Utah and Arctic testimony collections mentioned earlier, began the process of contacting potential contributors who could speak about wilderness in Nevada. She felt that a collection of wilderness testimonies might help to build bridges across the state's diverse and scattered population and might also bring some national recognition to the extraordinary beauty of this place—beauty that makes it hard to believe the federal government has deemed it a wasteland suitable for a nuclear waste repository.

Roberta brought the idea to Friends of Nevada Wilderness (www.nevadawilderness.org), and the organization has enthusiastically supported the project. She invited University of

Nevada, Reno, professor Scott Slovic, one of the central scholars in the lively field of contemporary environmental literature, to help her plan and refine the manuscript and to work with prospective publishers. The purpose of this book is to represent, from a diversity of perspectives that reflects the wide range of people who live in or visit this state, the meaning of "wilderness" in this place at this time. Historian William Cronan and philosopher J. Baird Callicott, among many others, have challenged American readers in recent years to think more carefully about virtues and limitations of the concept of "wilderness." *Wild Nevada* offers the voices and viewpoints of both supporters of formal "wilderness" designation and people compelled to quarrel with "wilderness" for philosophical and practical reasons. We hope the diverse perspectives collected here will be one of the book's real contributions to discussions of wilderness within the state and beyond.

Nevada

—————— ••◦⟨◯◯⟩◦•• ——————

ANN HAYMOND ZWINGER

My first real introduction to Nevada came not on the ground but flying *over* it at 12,000 feet. The terrain stretched like a hammock slung between the Sierra Nevada and the Rocky Mountains, a place of interior drainage where, according to John Charles Frémont in 1843, its rivers and creeks "have no connexion [*sic*] with the ocean, or the great rivers which flow into it." I watched a typical Great Basin landscape beneath the wing, a land surface like an old weather-beaten canvas tarp pleated with arroyos and tucked with mountains, left out in the sun and wind of too many millennia, leaving it tattered and wrinkled, a landscape of dried-up lakes and an infinity of sagebrush that, with its grayed, subtle colors, looked just half past autumn entering the winter of its life.

That is only somewhat the reality on the ground. You can drive across for hours without seeing much change, on a road that seems to go on forever toward a soft, smudged, and bleak horizon. But it's on the ground that this very sere bleakness becomes a thing of beauty—a formal, restrained beauty of structure rather than a surface beauty of bright cheerful colors and playful land forms. But there are, hidden away, small, surprising packets of color as vigorous and bright as a box of new crayons.

As a naturalist, I find the close-up, hands-on approach appealing. The big overview is all and well, but being near-sighted as I am, I cherish the individual secretive places that you can't get to from here, places learned over the years of traveling in Nevada on various writing assignments, those unexpected and isolated surprising places, the shuttered places that Nevada holds like a good poker hand, close to its chest. These places are never advertised by strings of blinking neon lights, never touted in tourist brochures. You have to look for them, for they are acquired tastes, rough-cut gems that reward you for taking the time to find them in that vast-ness of severe sameness.

The ones I know are about as different as places can be: otherworldly Ash Meadows; a burn area north of Winne-mucca, thick with wildflowers responding to the shot of nitrogen and phosphorus that fires inject into the ground; sand dunes piled up in unexpected sites like those near Tonopah or Sand Mountain outside of Fallon. In this arid state, there are large areas of water, from Pyramid Lake's wide turquoise surface to the sedge-fringed wetlands in the Lahontan Basin that once supported a rich life system for the Native Americans who lived there. And playas, those flatter-than-flat land forms left after a lake evaporated. This crazy variety seasons Nevada with the fragrance of sagebrush, the pungency of deer weed, the hollering blue of a western sky— endemic landscapes.

It's the particulars that tie me to the natural world, the feet-on-the-ground stability, the feel of a sagebrush twig in the hand, the sounds and aromas, the tactile landscape that I can absorb through my senses. I experienced Ash Meadows not as hot and dry as I expected, but chill and damp. Little mindless streams ran here and there, through alkali soil that only a limited variety of plants can abide.

Water here fits the Ancient Mariner's lament of "water, water, everywhere but nary a drop to drink." That's because salt is everywhere, in lacy white windrows that bound open patches where no plants grow, along trickling rivulets. Salt-bush, with its rustling papery seeds, flourishes. So do salt grass, leaf tips as stiff and prickly as a cactus spine, and ink-weed with short, fat leaves that are adapted to this saline swath of desert. Ash Meadows is a different kind of desert: It is not *lack* of water that makes it a desert, but water that is unusable for plants because of the load of salt it carries.

The streams here belong to a once-larger lake-and-stream system filled with water from the runoff of the last glaciers, waters that supported native fish and plants now in danger of extinction. Ash Meadows—drab, unlovely, lonesome—is the strongest argument for maintaining places that do not attract us with fancy vistas but with the subtle and lasting beauty of plants and animals that have adapted to its rigorous demands.

While you're there, look for the Amargosa toad, *Bufo nelsoni,* one of the vertebrates threatened by pumping, as well as the more famous series of tiny blue-eyed pupfish. When the ancient lake-and-river system produced by Pleistocene runoff began to dry up, many species were isolated and, over millennia, separated into different species. The Amargosa toad's head is narrower and its legs shorter than other toads, but beyond its physical appearance, very little is known about its habitat needs, other than the fact that the toads' presence and good health indicates a likewise healthy and well-functioning ecosystem. They belong to that unexplored interior world that may hold so many answers to so many questions, and only taking time to develop patient studies and learn patient facts can produce honest answers.

At Ash Meadows I first experienced that particular variety of wind that Mark Twain called the Washoe Zephyr that is "manufactured on the mountain-top for the occasion," holds office hours from two in the afternoon until two in the morning, and for these twelve hours the walker has to allow for it "or he will bring up a mile or two to leeward of the point he is aiming at." Nevada's wind's main duty seems to be to create dunes, yet I almost gave up finding the Tonopah Dunes because the weather was down in the weeds and visibility was the same as a London pea-soup fog. But by some chance of luck, they finally loomed up out of the dank and dark.

Happily that dimness discouraged some of the fat, round

resident pill bugs from seeking solace underground as they would at the first splash of sunshine. Only as clouds began to lift did these tiny creatures begin to nudge themselves beneath the sand. Hidden during the day, they maraud the dunes in the evening, siphoning moisture, finding enough nibbles to support a minuscule diet. They were just one of those delightful Nevada lagniappes that less-than-provident weather provides to a curious naturalist.

Sand Mountain, the dunes southeast of Fallon, is a spectacular opposite—not only extremely visible from a distance but aurally active, alive with dune buggies snarling up and down the slope and across the ridge top. The winds have swept up the sands from the Carson Desert into tidy mounds 400 feet high. Sand Mountain has a poetic clarity of shape, heaped in rolling mounds of pale beige sand, arranged in eloquent sine curves and huge undulant hills. The wind constantly rearranges the ridges and peaks, and sand buggy aficionados come from a long way away for the challenge. A boot stomp can set the dunes singing, described as a softly musical sound possible to hear only when the dune buggies are done snarling.

Not far away lies the Carson Sink, a nightmare of ashy white alkali soil that wagon caravans going west in the nineteenth century did anything to avoid. It supports only saltbush and winter-fat salt grass and halogeton with its fat, succulent leaves. At the edge lie the marshes where Lahontan Indians once made a lifestyle out of alkali bulrushes, cattails, and tules. Now draining and ditching has put almost 98 percent of the land into alfalfa. Still, the open ditches provide rich space for birds, a birdwatcher's paradise with white-faced ibis, snow geese, prairie falcons, northern harriers, pippits, and a lot more. Bring binoculars.

And then there are Nevada's elegantly beautiful pallid playas, terrain that caused Dr. James Schiel, a geologist on a nineteenth-century expedition, to write that "if the eye of a man of ancient Greece had seen this sight, he would have located the entrance to the underworld here." Once part of that greater water system, these now-dry lakes stretch like glazed saucers to the horizon, the epitome of flat. If they're dry, they are great hiking. If they're wet, they imbibe axles, sneakers, and decent dispositions.

Once I wandered onto the wet apron of one, curious about what looked like huge fish bones imbedded like icicles on the surface. They turned out to be long bony salt crystals. I tried to tread delicately, but the inevitable happened and I sank ankle-deep into an oozing muck that encapsulated each shoe with a couple pounds of wet clay. I struggled and lurched back to dry land, feeling like Frankenstein crossing the laboratory floor.

These hidden treasures, unique pockets of landscape that exist nowhere else, turn Nevada into a treasure hunt. Tucked away in this vastness of windblown steppe desert, available only to those who know where to find them, are plants and animals beautifully adapted to a difficult environment, with world enough and time aplenty to twitch genes into new combinations. Nevada is a laboratory of ongoing change, of what was and what is and some direction markers to what may be. Nevada is unique, full of beauty, and it tweaks the mind like the wind twitches the tules.

How could you not love this great vastness of Great Basin that endures that never-ending Nevada wind that sandpapers the world? How could you not love this place that is so beautiful simply because it is? When I wander these back lots of Nevada, my loyalty to the natural world becomes intensified, enriched. Simply one woman's path. It works for me. Long live the wind!

Finding the Space in the Heart

GARY SNYDER

I first saw it in the sixties,
driving a Volkswagen camper
with a fierce gay poet and a
lovely but dangerous girl with a husky voice,

we came down from Canada
on the dry east side of the ranges. Grand Coulee, Blue
Mountains, lava flow caves,
the Alvord desert—pronghorn ranges—
and the glittering obsidian-paved
dirt track toward Vya,
seldom-seen roads late September and
thick frost at dawn; then
follow a canyon and suddenly open to
        silvery flats that curved over the edge

        O, ah! The
        awareness of emptiness
        brings forth a heart of compassion!

We followed the rim of the playa
to a bar where the roads end
and over a pass into Pyramid Lake
from the Smoke Creek side,
by the ranches of wizards
who follow the tipi path.
The next day we reached San Francisco
in a time when it seemed
the world might head a new way.

And again, in the seventies, back from
Montana, I recklessly pulled off the highway
took a dirt track onto the flats,
got stuck—scared the kids—slept the night,
and the next day sucked free and went on.

Fifteen years passed. In the eighties
With my lover I went where the roads end.
Walked the hills for a day,
looked out where it all drops away,
discovered a path
of carved stone inscriptions tucked into the sagebrush

"Stomp out greed"
"The best things in life are not things"

words placed by an old desert sage.

Faint shorelines seen high on these slopes,
long gone Lake Lahontan,
cutthroat trout spirit in silt—
Columbian Mammoth bones
four hundred feet up on the wave-etched
     beach ledge; curly-horned
          desert sheep outlines pecked into the rock,

and turned the truck onto the playa
heading for know-not,
bone-gray dust boiling and billowing,
mile after mile, trackless and featureless,
let the car coast to a halt
on the crazed cracked
flat hard face where
winter snow spirals, and
summer sun bakes like a kiln.
Off nowhere, to be or not be,

     all equal, far reaches, no bounds.
     Sound swallowed away,
     no waters, no mountains, no
     bush no grass and
        because no grass

no shade but your shadow.
No flatness because no not-flatness.
No loss, no gain. So—
nothing in the way!
—the ground is the sky
the sky is the ground,
no place between, just

wind-whip breeze,
tent-mouth leeward,
time being here.
We meet heart to heart,
leg hard-twined to leg,
    with a kiss that goes to the bone.
Dawn sun comes straight in the eye. The tooth
of a far peak called King Lear.

Now in the nineties desert night
    —my lover's my wife—
old friends, old trucks, drawn around;
great arcs of kids on bikes out there in darkness
    no lights—just planet Venus glinting
by the calyx crescent moon,
and tasting grasshoppers roasted in a pan.

They all somehow swarm down here—
sons and daughters in the circle
eating grasshoppers grimacing,

singing sūtras for the insects in the wilderness,
—the wideness, the
foolish loving spaces

full of heart.

From *Mountains and Rivers Without End* (Washington, D.C.:
Counterpoint, 1996).

Getting to Know Her

BRIAN BEFFORT

Nevada is shy. As do many people, she guards her vulnerable sides with an unsociable personality. From the interstate, her sere mountains and valleys seem inhospitable and uninviting. Were she a high school student, her classmates might call her stuck-up and aloof.

She has softer, nurturing sides, but to find them you must ignore her harsher first impressions. You must leave the highway and slow down. You must wander, carry water, and harbor few expectations. Explore her peaks and canyons diligently. With luck and good timing, you'll learn her secrets and hear her stories.

Late one afternoon in early spring, I drove along the Northshore Road in Lake Mead National Recreation Area. The sun was sinking low; it was time to find a place to camp. Fiery orange Aztec sandstone outcrops and a black basalt ridgeline south of the road convinced me to pull over along the narrow shoulder. No road sign or parking lot told me to stop here. No trails led to overlooks or interpretive signs. The contour lines on my map hinted at nothing spectacular, but I thought perhaps that ridge to the south would be a good place to camp and watch the sun rise over Lake Mead.

I shouldered my pack; left car, asphalt, and civilization behind; and hiked through a low forest of creosote bushes, across a landscape that looked as it might have in the beginning, when the paint from the creator's hand was still wet. Despite a million people living an hour away in Las Vegas, humans had left no mark here; no footprints, scattered spent shotgun shells, or sun-faded beer cans anchored the terrain in history. The low sun draped red and gold across the western faces of the sandstone, while shadows stretched like taffy to the east.

· · ·

The bleached white skeleton of a horse lay among the rocks. Delicate grass pushed up through the eye socket. The pelvic bone lay nearby on red sandstone as though placed by Georgia O'Keeffe. A desert tortoise shell lay in the gravel of a rugged wash. Each hinted at hard life and slow death under hot sun.

I reached the top of the ridge after sunset. Stars were beginning to shine, competing with the electric glow of Las Vegas to the west. I slept on a saddle between two small peaks—a popular place, judging from the coyote trails and ample scat in the area.

Dawn revealed no view of the lake. Instead, a nameless valley a mile square, hidden from road and water by small ridges, was carpeted entirely with gold and purple. In late fall, perhaps early winter, an isolated rain had chosen this valley over the many that surrounded it and gave seeds dormant in the soil a reason to celebrate. The vibrant party was in full swing as the sun peeked over the horizon.

I ran down the wash and into a proclamation of color and smell prophesied in the Bible: "The wilderness and the waterless region will exult, and the desert plain will be joyful and blossom as the saffron. Without fail it will bloom, and it will really be joyful with joyousness and with glad crying out" (*Isaiah 35:1*). Lacking such eloquence, I repeated "Oh my God" over and over like a mantra and tried to record the species I saw blooming before me.

A few I knew, such as Mojave gold poppy and bright pink beavertail cactus, ground-hugging pink and white phlox, pale purple asters, and yellow ephedra. Most species, however, eluded identification with their complexity of shape and color. Some were less than an inch tall, displaying intricacy that would inspire a Swiss watchmaker. Others were tall, scraggly, and brash in their statements. Woefully ignorant of botany or taxonomy, I recorded characteristics that might enable me to identify them later with help from a guidebook: "Yellow, 1 foot tall, multiple flowers an inch across, with green hairy stalk"; "Purple, 6 inches tall, 1-inch lobed hairy leaves at bottom, ¼-inch flowers at top"; or "Yellow, 2 feet tall, like a poppy, smells like root beer."

In all, I differentiated more than thirty species of flowers in bloom; many more were pushing up green to bloom later.

Most remain a mystery to me despite my hours of paging through guidebooks back at home while recalling lines from Robert Frost's "A Passing Glimpse":

> Was something brushed across my mind
> That no one on earth will ever find?
> Heaven gives its glimpses only to those
> Not in position to look too close.

A week later, a botanist followed my directions to the valley and identified more than sixty species of flowers in bloom, giving them Latin names such as *chaenactis, cammisonia, escholzia, phacelia,* and *amsinkia.* These lyrical names capture the magnificence of the display no better than did my inept scribbles.

On any other day in any other season in most years, this valley would have remained unremarkable, no different from a thousand similar draws. Indeed, wildflower displays equally or more splendid bloom in countless other valleys and meadows.

Everyone deserves to experience beauty on such a scale. Part of me wishes I could take others there, especially those unable to hike over a ridge to do so. Beauty such as I witnessed can soften the hardest souls and spark the dullest minds.

Now the bloom has passed, and seeds once again wait in the dirt for the right combination of water and sun to wake them. Yet should there be a road into that valley the next time it blooms, the magic would be gone. It wouldn't be a surprise. Not every event can be planned or shared. Some can only be discovered.

Weeks after that hike, I stood in line at a supermarket and listened to a young couple discuss how ugly and boring Nevada gets once you leave Las Vegas. While they credited the CD players and air conditioning for getting them through their journey across Nevada, I flipped through a tabloid and smiled, because I knew her better.

Mountain Romance

PETER BRADLEY

> A world without wilderness is a cage.
> —DAVID BROWER

Jerry, Tony, and I spent the better part of a morning wandering up into the clouds and out of the cage. In time, a woodland of singleleaf pinyon, Utah juniper, littleleaf mahogany, and curlleaf mountain mahogany with an understory of paintbrush, bitterbrush, buckwheat, globemallow, ricegrass, prickly phlox, and sage surrounded us, each tree and flower with a story to tell. Like a seasoned Tibetan peering out over his plateau, an old juniper stood in defiance, facing the wind, bent and cracked with age, yet vital and strong, more than ready, even willing to live another thousand years. A Townsend's solitaire—handsome, dignified, and solitary relative of the robin and bluebird—heralded the gates of the wilderness. We could not see him, but his call was unmistakable. Rising from the mist, a vertical wall of limestone appeared, one thousand feet high and two miles wide.

We clawed and scratched our way up through loose talus, mahogany, dwarf juniper, and limber pine duff. Following our path, the only way through a crack in the giant limestone rim, was like threading the eye of a needle. Our destination that evening was a tiny flat spot on a ridgeline to the south, edging through this vast jumble of vertical mountain and impenetrable woodland. The heavy packs pulled at our shoulders, beckoning us backward into the abyss. Ancient trees held out lower branches, handholds, just as safe passage appeared impossible.

I rested in a standing position, attempting to lower my heart rate to something below 200 beats per minute, one boot firmly planted on the uphill side of a securely anchored, horizontal trunk of thriving mahogany, the other boot dangling above the open maw of the mountain. A mountain chickadee settled on a branch of the same tree, one foot from my face, eyes staring into mine. My *Chickadeean* was too rusty for me to translate his message, but I believe the little fellow was trying to communicate "What on earth are you? Do you come in peace? Get your stinking carcass off my land. Chickadee Chickadee Dee Dee"—the sort of things any honest property owner would say upon discovering an alien in the garden. Embarrassed, I said nothing.

On somewhat more level ground now, thirty degrees but still climbing, we were free to examine the rocks and soil that made our path. One could not move without stepping on sea fossils, perfect rock replicas of ancient marine life. In truth, the entire mountain range was one grand heap of carcasses deposited layer after layer in the warm, productive seas of the

Paleozoic Era, some 400 million years ago. Through the agency of plate tectonics, heat, pressure, faulting, erosion, and of course the passage of deep time, these marine fossils—brachiopods, crinoids, clams, sponges, and diatoms all underfoot—are now perched high up in a twenty-first-century Nevada, approximately 9,000 feet above current world sea level, in some of the driest landscape on the North American continent. And then, things started getting interesting. On north slope aspects of this behemoth—in cracks in the fossil bed, in flower gardens of saxifrage and alpine columbine—living relatives of shelled sea creatures crawl about, consuming nutrients and moisture directly from organic duff and fossil strata. Long ago, *Oreohelix loisae,* an endemic Nevada mountain snail, released its bonds to the sea and found refuge in the highest and wettest microclimes of Nevada's wilderness. While retaining an uncanny resemblance to a long line of sea creatures reaching back to the Cambrian oceans, the sea snails and cephalopods and their ilk, these land creatures about the size of a man's thumbnail, appear curiously well adapted to the rigors of life in the mountains—much more at home than, say, the ungainly bipedal visitors presently crashing and clanging their way up the mountain slope.

Bits and pieces of bagpipe music drifted in the breeze as we topped a saddle between two stately Engelmann spruce trees. Closer inspection established that the music was performed by the ruby-crowned kinglet and black-throated gray warbler who were defining their breeding territories for the weeks and months to come. Spectacular, robust, and complex vocalizations came from those tiny creatures—fat kinglets weigh in at only 6.5 grams. In comparison, the fat hiker weighed in at approximately 99,000 grams, and, sadly, I couldn't carry a tune.

The promise of flat ground lay just ahead. Camp, a small patch of horizontal ridgeline, presented itself just as evening began settling into the wilderness. Small patches of spring snow lay all about like heaps of diamonds deposited in bristlecone pine duff, manicured and cared for by as yet unseen elves and wood nymphs. Far more valuable than mere jewels, however, these patches provided drink and wash water, soup, snow cones, coffee, tea, lemonade, and ice rocks for our occasional ration of grog. Red-lavender sky reflected off red upturned roots of blow-down bristlecone and limber, deepening their color to crimson. Pairs of mountain bluebirds, males pure blue and females gray-blue, chatted and flitted about camp, seemingly unhappy with, though undaunted by, the intruding brutes. Apparently we had set our camp close to their wooden nest cavities.

While the sky-colored songbirds took turns scolding and lecturing us from various perches around camp, we made fire, water, and supper. The incense of burning cedar, the hot mahogany coals, our good health and full stomachs, hard uphill pulls, and leagues upon leagues of wilderness stretching hundreds of miles in all directions of the compass, each peak and ridge and valley lit in soft alpenglow, infused us with a deep and abiding peace. Eventually, birds and humans settled in together for the night.

A cold and biting wind kicked up and drove me to my sack where I lay staring straight up into the blackening night as Vega, Denab, and Polaris blinked on. I wondered how I could make it up to the three pairs of resident bluebirds huddled against the night in their wooden caves, probably deep in nightmare.

I woke at 2 AM. The sky was on fire with cosmic radiation, the mountain black as bituminous coal. I stood up in my long underwear, walked to rim's edge, and looked across those hundred miles. Not a streetlight, not a farm, not an all-terrain vehicle in sight; no motor to mar the night. This is as close as one can come in the Lower 48 to the frayed, ragged edge of human civilization. Sure, there was a road or two somewhere down in the blackness, but no one traveled them. There on the edge, I would commit to guard and defend the last of Nevada's wildlands, the remaining 20 percent or so, with all my heart and soul to the end of my days as a sort of last defense against Brower's ever-encroaching cage. Perhaps then, my little blue friends and their solitary cousins could find it in their hearts to forgive.

Back in the sack I fell into restful sleep, thinking about the basin big sage and green rabbitbrush widening the cracks of some forgotten highway in the valley below. Perhaps there is still hope for that other 80 percent, the area presently overrun by man and his machines.

Nevada

LINDA HUSSA

This Nevada land
　is nothing—

　　barren
　　nothingness of desert
　　only colors
　　first and last

This raised lava flow
　fierce, ripped, writhing in place
　dusted with million of years
　layer and layer of wind-blown, rain-carried, pulverized
　　rock
　not even soil
　mere infinitesimal bits sifted up
　and on this
　aspen where snows bank
　quivering as a sage grouse drumming

　is nothing.

Nevada

Knobs and lines of distant hills
   ink dipped in shading pale
   each form—in its own perfection
   within my sight

   nothing.

Breaks,
   short draws draining towards the Yellow Hills
   where stone-hard bones of Lahonton's fish
   Africa's elephant
   Arabia's camel
   Asia's redwood splintered on the sand—

   are nothing.

Shard litter of weapons
   broken stone tools
   around me where I am seated in the enormity of this place
   Earth's heat warming me
   that warmed others forgotten years gone
   bewildered ones who found themselves born here
   roamed, camped, killed, birthed
   starved, sorrowed
   found God, rejoiced God

all these nothing.

Piddling spring
   that springs
   from the gravel bed
   beneath a rock face raising to a raven's nest
   flows—has always flowed—for miles—more
   knowing least resistance
   sustaining, sustaining

   nothing.

That raven
   glistening black graceless bird
   flapping straight away
   watches time unfold

   and it is nothing.

Shy creatures
   feed, fly
   scuttle, scare
   slither, slip
   haltingly step, arrogantly march
   thunderous with conspicuous speed

nothing.

Sky in brightness
   opalized unearthly colors
   haughty, tauntingly stingy
   a fearsome boiling cauldron
   benevolent
   shadowed, calm
   translucent
   and in that great hollowness of night
   it becomes roan with stars
   expanding to source or destiny?

Silence
   the unshakable
   pierce of silence

   all nothing.

From *Blood Sister, I Am To These Fields* (Reno, NV: Black Rock Press, 2001).

Nevada Through the Eyes
of a Western Shoshone

LAURA RAINEY-CARPENTER

Indian people have lived in this area for over eight thousand years. They hunted deer, antelope, elk, sheep, goats, and bison. My ancestors from the Baker area would spend their winters down in Snake Valley, then take the Old Shoshone Trail which went up Baker Creek and dropped off over the summit into a beautiful meadow. It was lush with grass and wild flowers. The wild Iris was like a blue blanket on both sides of the stream that wandered through the valley. They spent their summers in the high meadow, gathering the wild onion, Yomba (wild potatoes), berries, and tea. They fished in the streams and snared rabbits and other small animals for variety. The deer dance was held at night before the hunt, and the deer was honored and thanked for the food and clothing he gave them. When nuts and berries and other items were gathered, an offering of sacred tobacco or something else was left for the land that gave so much to them.

Everyone was taught to respect all things, taught that Mother Earth and all her creatures were to be protected. The Indian way of thinking, in the past and today, is to take only what is needed and to never waste anything. They thanked the plants and animals for giving them sustenance. The Elders believe it more important to give than to receive. As my ancestors moved around the mountains gathering pine nuts, they would visit various pictograph and petroglyph sites. There are numerous sites painted or etched on vertical stone cliffs in the area. They have withstood thousands of winter snows and summer heat waves. Most of these are situated in locations where they tell stories of those areas. A person reading the stones could pick out various mountain peaks and streams in relation to the location of the paintings and etchings.

The "wilderness rape" which has been forced upon us has made it impossible for my eighty-eight-year-old mother and my two-year-old grandson to visit their aboriginal lands! The so-called "public lands" that should be available to *all* are now only available to a select few. The access roads that were there years ago are still there, but we are not allowed to use them. The trailhead to the Old Shoshone Trail has been obliterated so no one can use it. Someone decided to chip off some of the pictographs and set them alongside a "nature trail" near Baker Creek. In a matter of ten years, the figures had become virtually invisible because they were displayed horizontally, subjected to direct sun and weathering. Now the great "nature trail" consists of a parking lot and toilet!

When the Indians administered the land, they didn't need

wilderness designation. They used all areas to their advantage and preserved the land for future generations. We don't need more wilderness areas—we need to educate the non-Indian people to respect Mother Earth and all things connected.

Earth, Sky, Invincible Wild

ROBERT LEONARD REID

One or two evenings a week, just before retiring for the night, I step outside into my front yard. My neighbors kindly douse their porch lights soon after sundown, and quiet their dogs. Moments after I close the door behind me, the great Nevada wilderness sweeps me into its arms.

Above, in depths of space so deep they're scary, mysteries and omens barnstorm the heavens. Inscrutable mountains rise up around me, a coyote cries, the beguiling odor of sage fills the air, undocumented breezes report in from distant lands. Before long I'm smelling comets, I'm listening to spiders spinning their after-hours webs. My address is Carson City, but it might as well be a cozy cave in the Paleolithic.

Do I fear that wilderness is passing?

Not for a moment. It's true that for as long as I can remember, I've been decrying the assault on America's wildlands by the rapacious American consumption machine, and I'm not about to quit now. At a time when the nation's president views the Arctic National Wildlife Refuge as a nice place for an oil well, and the vice-president's idea of wilderness is a gun club without valet parking, we need vigilant defenders of the wild more than ever.

[43]

But in the transcendent quiet of a vast Nevada night, I'm rocked by a perception that sometimes eludes me during pedestrian daylight hours—a perception not of a withering landscape under final assault by a ruthless, indefatigable enemy, but of a vibrant, tolerant, and infinitely strong omnipresence waiting patiently for the world to come to its senses.

The idea of an invincible wilderness just beyond my doorstep is a new one for me. Before arriving in Nevada seven years ago, I viewed the wild as an exotic, fragile place to which I traveled after months of dreaming and planning—the Tetons, where I went to climb summer after summer, the Bugaboos, Shasta, the High Sierra. I'd load up my backpack and drive two or three days. Hooray! Wilderness!

In Nevada, where we're understocked in Top-10 thrills, such as the Tetons and the Bugaboos, but crammed to the rafters in the grandeur of the everyday, I've come to understand wilderness not as the stuff of *Arizona Highways* photographs but as the world I live in; not as spectacle but as air and sky and earth—as the taste and feel of Tuesday evening in my front yard. Here the veneer of civilization lies lightly over the landscape. On a sidewalk near the capitol building, indomitable desert plants press upward between the cracks. Ten minutes from my house I watch a team of badgers routing an unlucky ground squirrel's den. Turkey vultures cruise the skies; coyotes sun themselves in a nearby field, daydreaming of rabbit chops. My friend in Jacks Valley returns home at the end of the day to find a pair of bald eagles perched on the roof of his house. Do I worry that civilization is crowding in on eagles? Of course. But I'm happy to report that in Nevada, it's sometimes the other way around.

A Nevadan has an easy time understanding Robinson Jeffers's confidence in the steadfastness of nature. "It has all time," reflected the brooding poet of the Pacific in "Carmel Point":

> It knows the people are a tide
> That swells and in time will ebb, and all
> Their works dissolve. Meanwhile the image of the
>   pristine beauty
> Lives in the very grain of the granite,
> Safe as the endless ocean that climbs our cliff.

From *Selected Poems* (New York: Random House, 1987).

The people are a tide. For Jeffers, humans were the problem— all humans. Enraged by profit-driven development, he made the mistake of confusing the ravenous few with everyone else, and became an intolerable misanthrope. I wish he had known a few of the men and women who live on my street, who are not destroyers. Working-class one and all, they provide healthy antidotes to the bitterness and disengagement that come with living alone on a privileged rock, as Jeffers did, and a firm refutation of his thesis. They like unspoiled nature. They're kind to it. They walk their dogs in it. They fish it and hike it and swim it and picnic it. They turn off their porch lights at night and then go out and smell it. They believe in open space, and when a card-carrying ravager showed up recently to carve a BMX track into a cherished spread of sagebrush, we all joined forces to defeat the plan. I don't deny that my neighbors want their toys and their TVs; so do I. Americans, all of us, want and use too much. We need to work on this.

Meanwhile, it's time to trust each other again. Most Nevadans don't want to crush wild things. Wild things are in our hair and in our nostrils and in our dreams. Why should we crush them? Don't misunderstand me: We must have officially protected wilderness, the more of it the better. Keeping land wild today will simplify matters when the time comes to tear down the dams and bulldoze the malls.

But I'm tired of apologizing for wild country as though it were an old dog in need of a warm bed and a pat on the head. I'm fed up with smiling in a friendly manner and saying thank you for leftovers after Exxon, Georgia-Pacific, and Alcoa have taken their slices. I'm disturbed when advocates for wilderness argue for its protection on the basis of economics, history, recreation, science. Stop it! Say this to the senator: The world is wild and beautiful, and you'd damned well better see that it stays that way! Say this to the developers: Woe to you small-minded pinch-pennies, you pathetic asphalt fiends, you vandals and plunderers, you ridiculous self-important ones. Two weeks in the Ruby Mountains for you!

The future is in free-running rivers and snowy mountains and deserts so wide and so graceful they make you cry. The purpose of Nevada, where the wild and the beautiful are as familiar as day and night, is to remind the world of the primacy and goodness of wilderness as a moral principle, and of the will of the people to live in it and glory in it. Coexistence begins here.

A Chaos of Contingencies

ROBERT MCGINTY

I'm on a thin ridge as jagged as broken bone. It's August, a dry August in a dry year. No trails lead to this place a thousand feet above the canyon bottom. It's a good hour's climb through dense willow and stands of stunted aspen, then into the limber pine, then up a loose crumble of granite and across a slick-rock chute and onto a tumble of boulders the size of Volkswagens.

Just before I reach the top, a little mule deer buck bolts out of a bed at the base of a cliff and vanishes in three pogo-stick bounds. Fifty feet from the ridge line, the steep pitch of the canyon eases, curves. Plates of slatey rock cobble the ground and clatter under my feet like broken china.

On top, I take off my day pack. I've brought water, an apple, a book, a jacket. The back of my shirt is sweat-drenched, chilled in the breeze. I use the pack for a cushion and sit back against a large rock and look east. Beyond the chalk-white playa below I count five more mountain ranges, frozen like blue stone waves. Cloud shadows bruise the foothills. A Clark's nutcracker drops from the top of a dead pine, caws, and then flies to another lightning-seared snag, a good vantage point, too.

I often have reasons for coming to these mountains—to camp, to fish, to hunt. Often I come with a friend. Sometimes it's good to note things with another, to say "how beautiful" in a hundred different ways, or to say nothing at all.

Today I have no reason. Had I wanted to read my book, I could have found comfort closer to home. Since I've turned fifty, I take pleasure in just walking. If I'd only wanted to walk, I would have picked flatter terrain. I've lost my footing twice in the climb today and banged a knee bloody sliding down a steep slope.

The rock I sit against is scaled with lichen, orange and green and red. Dwarf asters bob near my feet, and a prickly cushion of white alpine phlox stitches itself into the exposed soil. A large, flat rock to my left is piled with marmot droppings.

I think of the image many have of my native state—a hot, barren, lifeless landscape suited best as a graveyard for junk cars and deadly isotopes. I think, too, of the metaphors often used to describe Nevada's abundant wilderness—jewels, gems, treasures. For some the appeal, ultimately, is to the pocketbook. Aren't treasures to be unearthed, their worth translated into the leisure and comfort that opulence allows? Sometimes, understandably, supporters of wilderness evoke tourist dollars and visitor days to justify preserving wild places, as if a price tag alone might confer protection. Without the slightest sense of irony, even the most anti-wilderness of chambers of commerce smatter their brochures with images of alpine lakes and remote basins dazzled by autumn aspens. Selling wilderness is sometimes big business.

But this ridge where I sit today is too thin, too spare for a postcard vista. It sells nothing, makes no promises, promotes no cause. It is neither benign nor malevolent. It neither invites nor spurns. It is, like all wilderness, a fragile defiance of the mania to control, to order, to conquer, to subdue. The best science we have could not have predicted its detail, and our best engineers could not replicate its design. The explanations of geologists and botanists and biologists are peripheral to the reality of this thin ridge, the flowers at my feet, the call of the nutcracker. And while I am here, I am a part of this place, this chaos of contingencies bound by beauty.

It will take me an hour to pick my way down the mountainside to the trail in the canyon bottom, and another hour down the canyon to the trailhead where I began. But it's still morning, and the day is long. I'll sit here for a while. From time to time a pika will call. I'll watch deer feeding below me, and at noon a flock of mountain bluebirds will whistle along the ridge. Tomorrow, and for weeks and months to come, the peace of this day will be a counterweight to the everyday turmoil and often petty demands of my life. And it will be an incentive to return and again be renewed.

Wilderness Point

———————•‹⟨∞⟩›•••———————

PATRICIA SWAIN

> You ask of my companions. Hills, sir, and the sundown,
> and a dog as large as myself . . . —EMILY DICKINSON

> If you got to ask, you ain't never gonna get to know.
> —attributed to LOUIS ARMSTRONG
> when asked to define "jazz"

> The Raccoon is the trickster, the sly and crafty. . . . The
> Raccoon is the survivor, who lives alongside man as if
> to show him that he cannot truly conquer the land. . . .
> —http://www.loomcom.com/raccoons/
> (The Worldwide Raccoon Web)

A raccoon frequently visits my garage. This gives me hope, hope for the natural world. I call him Wellstone, for he visited on the eve of the Minnesota senator's death. There is no surface water for miles. That does not stop him. He is considered a "varmint" in this state and subject to annihilation. That does not stop him. I live in a crowded subdivision. That does not stop him. He brings with him the whisper of forests, streams, lakes, trees, and the world beyond the freeway. There are more of his kind in neighboring California, but they are frequently sighted in Nevada as well.

Raccoons are among the oldest, wisest, and most adaptable inhabitants of our country. They were revered by Native Americans and early settlers. They were considered the national animal.

According to the Raccoon Rescue Web site: "Their intelligence level is that of primates. Their paws and toes identify objects as well as human hands. Raccoons provide a very important link in the chain of life. Without them, we would suffer an epidemic of vermin such as mice, rats, and snakes. Raccoons do not carry the rabies virus. It is caused from the bite of an infected animal that is shedding the virus" (http://www.raccoonrescue.com).

Even as civilization closes in on their remaining habitat, even as 2–4 million are killed for their pelts annually—and as cars kill many more—this animal's numbers increase. It occupies most of North America, then its niche is filled by the coatimundi in Mexico and Central America. With his amazing adaptability and resilience, the raccoon gets my vote for wilderness poster child, followed closely by the coyote.

Wellstone has been here since 2000, as my dog's sniffings, and the empty cat bowls and torn cat-food bags plainly attest. I know where he hides, but he's only let me see him twice. That's fine. I'm happy just to know he's thriving.

It's the same with wilderness. I'm happy just to know it's out there and it's thriving. I'm happy knowing that on November 6, 2002, the Clark County Conservation of Public Land and Natural Resources Act of 2002 was officially signed into law, which meant eighteen new wilderness areas totaling 452,000 acres were added into the National Wilderness Preservation System.

I do not need to set foot upon it to fully rejoice in its existence. I need only know it is there. I do not need to subjugate Wellstone as though he is a dog. I need only know he is there. Raccoons raise themselves without any leashes, muzzles, choke collars, shock collars, surgery, daycare centers, or birthday parties. He does not need to serve me. Open, unsullied land does not need to meet my economic needs. Its existence fulfills my spiritual needs.

But, upon reflection, I realize the reason I can rejoice in the existence of additional official wilderness and in the unofficial visits from Wellstone is because I have experienced both in my life. Because I have known hours and days in the vast quiet and because I have lived in a crumbling wreck of an old farmhouse with a raccoon, I can carry the wilderness within me. I cannot supply this knowledge for anybody else. I can just preach to the choir about the importance of wilderness and, if any converts come along, that is added value.

Wilderness, in its broadest definition, is anywhere the quiet descends both within and without. Wilderness is that place where there are no works of man and only that which spontaneously arises without man's interference exists. Wilderness is wildness. And wildness means man is not in control. For some of us this spells joy, fascination, and discovery even if tinged with danger. For others this means fear, threat, competition, and loss.

Recently I hiked with my sister and young nephew. He was fine, chattering away, until we reached a point where the road noise fell away and there we encountered no other people. A long trail wound before us, gradually ascending, circling the mountain. Two vultures rode thermals overhead. "Mommy," he said, "we have to go back. We go back now. We don't know where the car is." This was his Wilderness Point.

Walking with a very civilized friend in hills near my house, we were chatting. But as we went farther, it got quieter. Quiet is the first signal. Later come the discoveries and realizations. Distractions float away. "Are there cougars out here?" she asked, with visible discomfort. Wilderness Point for her.

My pet raccoon recognized the sound of my mother's car approaching. He would hide under her chair, chuckling and rubbing his hands together in glee. (Live with a raccoon, and you will observe the animal rubbing its hands and chuckling.) When she sat, he sprang, grabbing her ankles. He got his payoff every time, as she jumped up and screamed, "Get that animal out of here!" The raccoon in me did not comply. This was her Wilderness Point. She hated the raccoon because she feared him; I could never convince her he was harmless.

Does everything in the world have to be on the grid and standardized? Do all our pets need obedience training? Can more of us learn to recognize and welcome our Wilderness Point, that hairy edge between the familiar and the unbounded and unknown?

When I came west, the treeless moonscape attracted at first in a perverse manner; like a Diane Arbus photo or a mummy from the pages of *Ripley's Believe It or Not*. I looked out the window in shock. "This isn't right," I said. It was my Wilderness Point.

The desert is landscape gone naked, most unnatural to the Easterner. It took a few years to love it. There is no tangle of undergrowth to hide the bare land, and each bush remains an isolationist distance from the next. It lures one into its depths because the footing is so easy and, in the vastness, faraway hills seem closer than they turn out to be. In the quiet, one is absorbed in the thought flow and time eclipses. One cannot escape the meditative state. Spotting a pile of rusted cans or a yellowing old photograph blown against a sagebrush root is a shock to the system. If a car approaches, it is like an earthquake to the senses.

My first Nevada memory: standing on a hill near a deserted ranch outside Austin. All I could hear was the blood circulating in my ears. I had been on a loosely defined spiritual quest, and this was its realization. A new level of peace enfolded me. Here was more contiguous wildland than I had ever experienced. From these many acres descends the peace. It cannot be duplicated where road noise or gunshots or any machines interfere.

My refuge these days is a scant half-mile from my house. Although smaller than that initial vista in central Nevada, it is big enough for the peace to exist. And that is the beauty of Nevada, that is this state's riot of wealth—that so close in we have trails, peaks, stones for perching and meditating, cool shade of junipers, fragrance of bitterbrush and sage, magpies, jackrabbits and cottontail rabbits, the occasional coyote, red-tailed hawks, mountain bluebirds, scrub jays, barn owls, a couple of rufous-sided towhees, California quail, Western fence lizards, horned lizards, blue-belly skinks, rattlesnakes, garter snakes, bull snakes, and more. And rarely any other people. Even other Nevadans do not take advantage of all this. Most people stick to the parks and playgrounds, the ball games, the noise, and each other. I like to imagine the impact so much wild land would have on New Yorkers I have known, some of whom flee in terror at the sight of a cow.

Often-traveled trails never bore because they are never the same twice. New streams flow after the rare storms, leaving braided trails. A coyote's voice drifts on a distant wind. In early spring the desert paintbrush, the sego lilies, the green ephedra, the wild onions, the death camas, the desert buckwheat, the Russian thistle, prickly poppy, tumbling mustard, lupine, globemallow, blazing star, prickly pear, phlox, daisies, rabbitbrush, arrow-leaf balsamroot—and more whose names I do not know—gradually bow in. One day I discover that unseen hands have cleared a path up the tallest peak and built a stone cairn, strange and foreboding. One spring I literally reel to the ground with the intoxication of it all. Snow changes everything yet again. The clouds, the sky, and the colors are always new.

There is enough variety and interest in this local area to provide a satisfactory experience, but there is also the pervasive knowledge that soon paved roads will intersect and more subdivisions will invade and all will be lost. I attend enough neighborhood meetings to know this is inevitable. We need legal protection for our lands because these neighborhood retreats can and will disappear, and only the big public holdings will be left for us.

If the day comes when raccoons cannot even find friendly garages to raid, when all closes up and closes in, there will be no Wilderness Point to reach, and we will be vastly impoverished.

I Kneel to See the Dead Great Horned Owl

GARY SHORT

found on the shoulder of the road.
This morning its night eyes are still
open and oval as a citron moon animated
like the glass eye of a Buddha.
The owl's on its back

on a bed of red dirt—Manet's
dead matador, one wing a gray cape
thrown nakedly open
to an absence in the sky. I think of
the luff of owl wings,
the last swoop and glide
before it was struck by a truck
and slammed into its own shadow
with a plush thud in the roadside dust.

Now I regard the owl, and it
seems to regard me. The longer I look
the more I'm reminded
of Severn's pencil drawing

of the vulnerable Keats,
very peaceably asleep, forever.

Aren't the dead always waiting
to be lifted? With both hands
I take the soft bird body,
heavier, more dense
than I might have guessed,
and carry it to the car, placing the owl
next to me in the seat of the passenger.

. . .

My friend Diane makes three paintings
and one drawing of the owl in two days.
But now the yellow moons of the eyes
are eclipsed and she asks me
to take the owl, which she has kept
in the refrigerator with a head of lettuce
and rolls of film. Since I've found him
there have been odd juxtapositions,
the owl where it should not be:
on the ground, on the car seat next to me,
and now again in Diane's refrigerator.
Lettuce is to film as owl is to wind.

[59]

And so I want to put the owl where it belongs.

In a tree, I'm thinking, shouldn't an owl be
in a tree? It is an old oak—gray, weathered,
bare. But still there
on the edge of my neighbor's ranch, still the tallest thing
for miles among the sage, stunted pine and juniper.

The skewed and relic oak to which all owls in the valley
will come in their time.

Where I live, I've heard the great-horned owls
and their call that is a question.
Like the coyotes they are often heard but seldom seen.
On a windy September day I hike for an hour,
cradling the owl until I reach the bleached-gray tree.
The oak has been dead for years.
The limbs brittle
like bleached coral. Where two limbs cross
I take baling wire and twine to secure the owl,
with difficulty, upright in the tree.
The wind swaying through the grasses
sounding like the river that isn't here.

• • •

I Kneel to See the Dead Great Horned Owl

Absence has its own sound.
One day at dusk I heard it
and began to walk toward the relic oak.
Three weeks since I left the owl in the tree.

The sun was setting along the ragged ridgeline,
a bright glow like burning
paper. The low clouds were red with flame.
I skirted the old mine, its beat-up, second-hand land
where the earth is torn
inside out, a shamble of gray tailings. Then
followed the trail that zigzags
along the wash and jags across the gully
traced by summer rains. A bright
and swollen moon,
nearly full but a bit wobbly, was on the rise.

A few white asterisks began to show in the sky.
I climbed out of the ravine
and approached the tree, but was stopped
by confusions of light that puzzled
for some moments
before I realized what I was seeing.
A thousand and another thousand
feathers blown loose from the owl,

caught and leafed out
from each taloned twig and limb.
The tree was filled with feathers of silver
that pulsed and thrilled. The mind of the owl tree
was plural, every feather
a separate flight, shining to live.

Nevada: Wilderness or Wasteland?

JON CHRISTENSEN

The words we choose have power on the wild land. And over the years, words have not been kind to Nevada's deserts. Even John Muir, that connoisseur of the wild, was hard on Nevada. But then Nevada was hard on John Muir. "When the traveler from California has crossed the Sierra and gone a little way down the eastern flank, the woods come to an end about as suddenly and completely as if, going westward, he had reached the ocean," Muir wrote during a trip to Nevada in 1878. "From the very noblest forests in the world he emerges into free sunshine and dead alkaline levels. Mountains are seen beyond, rising in bewildering abundance, range beyond range. But however closely we have been accustomed to associate forests and mountains, these always present a singularly barren aspect, gray and forbidding and shadeless, like heaps of ashes dumped from the sky."

I don't mean to quarrel with John Muir. . . . well, perhaps a little, for I find him a provocative foil. Like Muir, and like many Nevadans, I too came from California to Nevada. But I stayed and fell in love with Nevada's secrets—which are often hidden in plain sight. It just takes a while to see them, and perhaps even longer to give them the right name. It was from atop the Sierra, looking east, that Muir formed his first impression of Nevada. The state, Muir acknowledged, had generously productive gardens, grain fields, and hayfields, but from his preferred perspective, high on a mountaintop, arid valleys filled the picture. Green fields were "mere specks lying inconspicuously here and there, in out-of-the-way places," he wrote in a series of essays for a California newspaper. "To the farmer who comes to this thirsty land from beneath rainy skies, Nevada seems one vast desert, all sage and sand, hopelessly irredeemable now and forever."

First impressions are telling. And in Muir's writings, we find the two images that continue to define Nevada's wildness: the "bewildering" repetition of basin and range, basin and range, basin and range, like waves on an endless ocean; and the vastness of the "irredeemable" desert. And so the wilderness and the wasteland—two words whose meanings have been entangled throughout their history—were joined from the beginning in Nevada. The first definition of a "wasteland" in the *Oxford English Dictionary* is "land in its natural, uncultivated state," especially "a waterless or treeless region, a desert." "Wilderness" too is defined as "wild or uncultivated land" and "a waste or desolate region of any kind," but also "something figured as a region of a wild or desolate character, or in which one wanders or loses one's way; in religious use applied to the present world or life as contrasted with heaven or the future life." And so we begin to get a hint of the redemption possible in wilderness and even in the wasteland, as they blend together and become metaphors for life itself—not just life in its beneficent, embracing, nurturing sense, but life as difficult, harsh, challenging, necessarily risky, and, yes, even dangerous. And that, I think, gets pretty close to life in the wilds of Nevada.

Of course, the meanings of words change over time. And that can change the way we see the land. That, in turn, can change the way we treat the land. And that can then change the land.

In the 1980s, a century after Muir traveled across Nevada, a bumper sticker began appearing on vehicles traveling the state's lonely highways and back roads. "Nevada is not a wasteland," it asserted in the face of the federal government's relentless efforts to entomb high-level nuclear waste in the Nevada desert. The creation of Great Basin National Park and the designation of fourteen wilderness areas on mountain ranges across the state signaled a growing sense of separation between the wasteland and wilderness. The two no longer meant the same thing. Wilderness was something special and rare in the wasteland.

It was among the bristlecone pines high on a mountain that John Muir understood this, that the rarity of life in the desert conveys its own special value. "But wheresoever we may venture to go in all this good world, nature is ever found richer and more beautiful than she seems," Muir wrote in the one

essay from Nevada that brims with the sublime love he generally reserved for places other than the desert. "And nowhere
may you meet with more varied and delightful surprises than
in the byways and recesses of this sublime wilderness," Muir
wrote of Nevada's mountain island forests, "scant and rare as
compared with the immeasurable exuberance of California,
but still amply sufficient throughout the barest deserts for a
clear manifestation of God's love."

Now we turn to the "barest deserts" and ask ourselves
whether these are wilderness or wasteland, or something else
we have yet to name. I have faith that Nevada, the wasteland
and the wilderness, can yet be redeemed by people who stick
around and learn to share its secrets. Just as John Muir learned
over time.

"Nevada is beautiful in her wildness," Muir concluded on
his trek through the state, "and if tillers of the soil can thus be
brought to see that possibly nature may have other uses even
for rich soil besides the feeding of human beings, then will
these foodless deserts have taught a fine lesson."

A Love Affair With Nevada

MARGE SILL

My love affair with Nevada began in 1953. My husband and I, like pioneers of old, were making our way slowly from the flatlands of Nebraska to return to the golden hills of California. However, our mode of transportation was not an oxen cart but an old Ford, dubbed "the Blue Monster," which sometimes ran and sometimes stopped. When we crossed into Nevada from Utah, the Monster seemed to feel at home and, rejuvenated, found its way into the canyons of the South Snake Range. We camped at Upper Lehman Creek among the pines and shimmering aspen, with the sweet sound of water soothing our ears and the faint scent of skunk permeating the air.

The next morning we found an ancient mountain mahogany and a trail that led upward. Shouldering our packs, we began to climb. We reached the shores of a small lake surrounded by meadow that was beginning to take on its autumn colors of gold and red. We were alone, surrounded by beauty, a few curious chipmunks, and an occasional mule deer. Obviously, hunting season had not begun.

The following morning we climbed the highest mountain we could see to what seemed like the top of the world—we later learned it was Wheeler Peak. I think we could see at least

200 miles in any direction, a view that made me so dizzy I had to lie down. When we finally descended, we explored the bristlecones, the glacier, the meadows. And then we had to continue our journey west to civilization, but we knew we would be back.

When we moved to Reno in 1959, our first thought was to explore the state we would call our home. Mt. Rose, just outside of the city, was the obvious place to start. Thirty times in forty years I climbed the mountain, always seeing new vistas, new rocks, new flowers. In the spring of 1960 we went to the Black Rock Desert and High Rock Canyon to learn about the high desert country of northwest Nevada and to trace the Applegate Trail. We returned there spring after spring.

In 1964 the Wilderness Act was passed, and Jarbidge became the first Nevada wilderness. Named after the Indian word for the "monster that lurks in the canyon," its waters flow into the Snake River of Idaho and eventually into the Columbia River and the Pacific Ocean. On our summer excursions to this country of the pointed firs, we found stone records of ancient peoples and an intoxicating variety of wildflowers as we explored canyon after canyon.

But it was Highway 50 that to me became the lifeline of Nevada. From the eight mountain passes as one drove east from Reno to Ely, you could see the magnificent Toiyabe Range, the slopes of Mt. Jefferson to the south, the massive structure of the Monitor Range, and a series of other ranges waiting on the horizon to be explored. Perhaps my favorite sight was on the road from Ely to Baker, a view of the white limestone cliffs of Mt. Washington and the distinguished bulk of Wheeler Peak. Year after year I came back to my initial love.

In the fifty years that have ensued since I first discovered Nevada, I have seen many changes, but the wildness of this place remains. The state now boasts over two million acres of designated wilderness because of the small number of dedicated people who worked to achieve this victory. Great Basin National Park, the only national park in Nevada, was established in 1986, protecting Wheeler Peak and its surroundings for all time. Nevada is no longer the "black hole" of the West, and discerning pioneers are coming to the state to experience its subtle beauty and the magnificent solitude of the present-day wilderness and the wilderness to be designated in the future. As Walkin' Jim Stoltz put it, "Let it stay, forever wild."

If We Care, and If We Dare

ANN RONALD

Flattening the folds of an old 1986 State of Nevada Wilderness Status Map, I finger the colored paper. The green of designated wilderness is only a tiny blip in the northeast corner. The orange of lands "administratively endorsed as suitable" mark two slightly larger squares that since have become National Wildlife Preserves, north and south. I trace scattered chunks of white, the cities and towns where urban Nevadans dwell, and then the solemn gray of "military reservations," dominating the other rainbow squares. Blended cream and khaki and green cover most of the rest of the state, "other lands" that belong to the federal government and fill in the blanks. Finally, I touch the deep yellows dotted sporadically here and there, the "wilderness study areas," places still under consideration, disproportionately small tracts of land we may still be able to preserve.

A newer 1992 map looks slightly different. More white for urban area, especially in Clark County and south of Reno (ironically, the Nevada Test Site now is white, too). A few more wilderness greens, though not nearly enough. The same military grays, expanded a bit. (I wonder, Will a 2020 map paint Yucca Mountain fireball red?) A slightly larger smattering of "suitable" oranges. The same deep yellows, still being studied, still being debated, still the source of quarrels, still unprotected even as our population grows and grows.

Deep yellows and suitable oranges on faded maps do not do justice to a "wilderness study area," nor does the term "wilderness study" accurately define what's really there. Closing my eyes, I picture scenes and scenery that might still be saved for our children—if we care, and if we dare.

Figured Indian peckings and carvings cover a wall of red sandstone as high and wide as the front of a two-bedroom house. Spirals and squares, handprints, snake-like squiggles, fully formed bighorn sheep dancing across a black stain of desert varnish—all this, and more, etched hundreds of years ago.

Another wall of burnt umber, broken by weather and erosion, rises from an apparently waterless wash. A pair of bighorn sheep, not etched but alive and moving fast, clamor straight up a narrow slot, their hooves scrabbling on the stone, dust spilling into the air.

Below them, not dry after all, the sporadic streamed hosts reeds and grasses turning bright green in the springtime warmth. A phainopepla flies in and out of a prickly acacia bush, building a nest alongside a tangle of mistletoe that flowers pale pinkish-white. Nearby, another coal-black cardinal look-alike flashes against the clouds and skitters into the acacia, too.

In another arroyo carved by winter runoff, a miniscule desert garden of flowers stipples the ground. Not one of the blossoms, the yellows and whites and purples, is larger than my little fingernail, but the drainage is absolutely awash in color. That's close up. From a distance, the ground resembles a jigsaw puzzle of volcanic black and brown.

But the Nevada desert isn't always dry. In the heat of summer, a sudden cloudburst sends a tirade of muddy water and red rocks tumbling end over end down an otherwise arid track. The accompanying noise, as loud as a jumbo jet revving its engines, ricochets off the steep canyon walls. I watch from an aerie perch, astonished by the unleashed power.

Then the clouds disperse in a powdery chiaroscuro of gray and gold. Sun streaks stretch from the sky to the ground in a tableau reminiscent of a medieval church window. The sun itself, a fiery ball of molten orange, sinks behind a black-brown chocolate ridge of stone.

Once, in the midst of a fierce display of lightning in northern Nevada, I watched a strand of pelicans, strung out like a pearl and onyx necklace, sway back and forth in the gathering dusk. They looked ghostly and ephemeral, almost unreal as they turned and twisted—first light, then dark, then light, then dark again.

December and January snow, settling on the piñon pine and mountain mahogany, paints Nevada peaks a soft brush of egg-shell white, turning them into Christmas card caricatures. Drifts fill the draws, coat the sharply corniced ridges. From a distance, the ranges look like Switzerland; closer, a proverbial wonderland tracked only by rabbits and voles, hunting coyotes and perhaps an occasional elk.

Then it's springtime. Dozens of yellow-headed blackbirds flock to a desert oasis. Swaying in the reeds, a careful three or four feet apart, each one tries to sing his heart out. The females, hidden in the rushes, sit on their nests and listen to the raucous chorus above their heads. Across the pond, a great blue heron lumbers into the sky, an awkward giraffe-of-a-bird until it's airborne. Suddenly, head-tip and tail extended, it becomes a stealth bomber of a bird, all purpose and poise.

At midnight, a long-eared owl hoots faintly into darkness. Another owl replies, softly. Otherwise, dead silence—silence so absolute that it's impossible to describe to a city dweller used to a constant undertone of voices and cars. Overhead, the Milky Way glimmers like a star-ship chandelier, its multiple constellations a glittered blur of light. One empty planet, Venus I think, looks across the galaxies at teeming earth. Here, in what surely must be wilderness, the noise of commerce seems very far away.

Resting in the faint shadow of a convoluted Joshua tree, I look up to see the contrail of an Army jet, the only sign of modernity, disintegrating overhead. Otherwise, the scene looks as it must have looked a hundred years before, with the subtle desert colors of cream and khaki and beige and brown —the bureaucratic colors of the Wilderness Status Map—and the vibrant rainbow colors of what we might save for our children, and for our grandchildren—if we care, and if we dare.

The Future of the Great Basin

MICHAEL P. COHEN

Sometime late in the afternoon you might be driving down a good two-lane road. Not another car is in sight. Never mind the highway sign that calls this road an extra-terrestrial highway. This land is so open, so uninhabited, it seems like the original *terra firma,* the skeleton and bare bones of the earth. You can see a hundred miles across the violet shadows creeping into a long valley, to a new range of mountains and a ridge line so mysterious and fascinating that you are surprised you have never gone there before.

Certainly the Great Basin contains more ranges of mountains than any one person can ever know, and like all ranges, each one suggests the origin of the earth. But this range has such a distinctive shape that you are sure you have never seen it before. You stop the car, consult the map, and realize that you were walking up a canyon on the other side of the ridge only a few months ago. You have driven this road scores of times but have never seen the geography in this light before.

Set apart by a distinctive geology and biogeography, scarred by its recent human history, this region tests human perception, tricks human memory, and divines human desire. And you must have a long memory to think of the region beyond its most recent past, because the past five decades of human behavior here include ultimate human horrors. Yet this land has been inhabited for a longer time, by cultures and biota that preceded the Europeans who have turned it to their own strange military needs.

Modern Americans have been here for such a short time, have experienced such a limited range of conditions, and have asked such paltry questions! Coming here in the midst of an interglacial era, what they have seen in the Great Basin is a forbidding climate, a cold desert, exposed minerals, a few shrubs and grasses, and empty space. Not long ago a paleo-ecologist patiently explained to me a simple fact: The earth has spent 90 percent of the last two million years in glacial eras; and during those times, the Great Basin valleys and mountains were the home of alpine forests. These two million years probably included about ten complete climate cycles. The climate of the present represents only about 10 percent of recent history. Our era is, in other words, neither representative nor final.

Add the following fact: Modern humans have been on this earth for about 100,000 years, and evidence of modern humans in the Great Basin is certain from only about 11,500 years ago. Humans have inhabited the earth through less than half of one glacial cycle. This is relevant to any future we might imagine for the region or ourselves.

Because the Great Basin seems to be mostly empty space, its future has been highly contested. It has been claimed most recently by traditional patterns of exploitation. The booming and busting mining eras of the past 150 years have left and are still creating monuments to a simple theory of history: People find only what they seek; the narrow economic questions they ask determine the limited answers they get. The ranching history of the past century leaves its own legacy of conflict between memory and desire: After permanently altering the grasslands of the region, ranching continues to hang on as a marginal occupation. The military history of the region has been most dramatic and most recent, a textbook example of the human mind confronting empty space as a repository for its worst nightmares. The idea of the Great Basin as a patchwork of bombing ranges, nuclear reserves, and secret installations comes from the earliest idea of the region as a place of no exit, where everything flows in and nothing flows out. The "M-X Missile System" of the early 1980s, the ultimate expression of this idea, proposed to make the entire region a nuclear target, capable of absorbing the weaponry of an "evil empire."

The Great Basin is not an empty repository, but an archive of natural and human history—full of all the wonderful and horrible things that make it a stark and complete picture of the world and of human ingenuity at work on the world. The results of military occupation must be preserved because they tell us about ourselves, but the real and viable future for the region resides in its natural history and natural beauty. An open and visible geology makes each mountain range a textbook for the study of the discipline, revealing the meaning of geology as space.

The biological history of the region has its own fascination. Here, for instance, bristlecone pines grow at high altitudes on limestone ranges, the world's oldest living trees. The tree-rings of old bristlecones, living and dead, embody ten thousand years of natural history, making the forests an archive or a window into the climatic history of the entire post-glacial era. The trees provide a record of terrestrial conditions for the region that is of the same temporal span as human occupation. But the bristlecone has, in the past forty years, acquired a value as modern sculpture. Now the old groves are preserved as exquisite and priceless sculpture gardens.

Here is what we might have learned late in the twentieth century, from our recent devaluation of nuclear weapons and our re-evaluation of bristlecone pines. A portion of the earth thought a desolate wasteland by one ignorant generation will become highly valued by the next, if the next generation grows wiser. The Great Basin is, at this very moment, on the cusp of such a transition of thought. Nobody would imagine this region to be an Eden, yet it no longer seems a desolate wasteland. We begin to notice that it is full of things that make it what it is. People come here in increasing numbers, attracted by its wild beauty, but hardly knowing yet what attracts them.

Dust Storms Sing

⌖

STEPHEN TRIMBLE

We worked our way across sagebrush-covered hills, my teen-aged daughter and I, leaving U.S. 395 in California on a 100-degree July day and crossing into Nevada along the old emigrant Noble's Cutoff that followed the willowed banks of Smoke Creek. At the rim of the Smoke Creek Desert playa, the sky turned black, the wind gusting hard.

Yellow-brown curtains touched down on the floor of the desert. We couldn't decide if we were looking at rain or dust, but we kept driving closer, up and around the north end of the dry lake, bumping along past ranches but still alone on the road, clocking eighty miles without meeting another vehicle.

The dust clouds closed over us. Playa dust is so fine and alkaline that the particles suspend in the air. The cold rain spattered us as we stepped outside, the hot wind held us up when we surrendered to it, and we breathed in shallow, acrid gasps.

We drove a little farther, creeping, lights on. As the wind shifted, the sky darkened, from yellow-brown shot through with light to a biblical darkness that moved over us with overwhelming authority. Visibility dropped to zero, and we pulled off the road to wait it out, kin to those farm families in Dust

Bowl pictures leaning into the wind as they retreated to their tornado cellars.

Within a few minutes, the cloud lifted a bit. We drove on. Dust draperies brushed past us in waves, but lulls in their wake gave us glimpses of the sky. With these fleeting panes of light and with our arrival on pavement, the intensity of the experience began to ease. Suddenly, a marker loomed along the dim roadside: "Planet X Pottery." We had stopped here together once before, and we were intent on stopping here again, storm or no storm.

The sign said, "OPEN."

Here, master potter John Bogard has lived for thirty years in one of the West's truly remote corners, in the canyon between the Smoke Creek and Black Rock deserts. The café in nearby Gerlach has it right: Ball cap patches brag on the place—"Gerlach, Nevada: Where the pavement ends and the West begins." From this spot at the end of the road, Bogard sells to clients from all over the world. His work fills several funky gallery rooms, and seconds are stacked on shelves in his dirt courtyard. People come from San Francisco and beyond just to purchase his fine-art pieces. You can even find him on the World Wide Web.

We found Bogard striding across his courtyard after moving some pieces inside—his only concession to the violence of the weather. He then retreated to a chair on a porch, watching gleefully as the winds pruned branches from his cottonwoods, sending them crashing down into his courtyard. He told us that this sort of storm was not uncommon; we were impressed by his calm. Though exhilarating, the drama of the afternoon felt more or less like the end of the world to us. We paid for two mugs that felt just right in the hand and left him, smiling placidly into the teeth of the storm, watching for more death leaps by branches of his shearing trees.

The wilderness that Bogard gloried in—the wilderness blowing from the desert into his dooryard—hovers in the Nevada air, with or without wind and storm. In gentler landscapes, friendly moisture disperses in the air over farmland. Arable land has a workmanlike fecundity—nothing radical, nothing extreme—that gives the green Midwest or the mid-Atlantic states a comfortable, civilized feel. But as your tongue shifts from those softer "M"'s to the sharper "N" of Nevada, to the "D" of desert, a clarity and cleanness take over.

This power, this desert wildness, blows through Nevada. We felt it in the dust storm; John Bogard lives with it.

The paradox is this: from Interstate 80, at 75 miles an hour, everything appears the same. And yet, in this spare and still landscape, when wildness uncoils, we take notice. Every thundercloud matters in the desert. Every grassy wind shimmer in the bunched wild rye matters. When crossing into our fields of vision, every jackrabbit, every raven, every leopard lizard, every California sister butterfly brings life and wildness and movement—a metaphorical pebble dropped into stillness, the living mirror of the pure and glorious opening arpeggio of a cello suite or piano sonata stirring the silence.

Stars still bring fire to the dark night skies. The geologic story—the tectonic drama of basin and range—animates the landscape with a force that keeps fundamental truths a part of daily life.

The power of wild Nevada reaches along dirt roads threading the centers of basins, stubbing into creeks and canyons to ghost towns and trout streams, tying together the pastures with the peaks. Tentative beachheads of culture and commerce—barbed fence lines, cows, a dust plume kicked up by a jouncing pickup, solitary ranches and gas station/casinos—lack sufficient force here to overrule the wildness of a basin and its attending mountains.

Nevada wilderness advocates must address dual illusions generated by the paradox of the desert—that there really isn't anything of consequence at all out there, or, if there is, little urgency exists, because Nevada is so wild that we need not rush to designate wilderness.

The first illusion is easiest to banish, for Nevada is a treasure of wild diversity and vivid life. Just slip away from that deadening interstate highway corridor. The character of the land shifts from basin to range as the woven bands of a Navajo rug vary in texture and hue. From lower elevation to higher, distinct wild places succeed one another, from the ocean of sagebrush that fills basins to the wildflowered understory of a mountain mahogany grove on the slope of an arid mountain.

Above, on austere limestone ridges where few other plants survive, Great Basin bristlecone pines while away the centuries. Like the desert itself, the bristlecones look dead—their wood dense with resin, sculpted by wind to the form and texture of stone—but they have simply chosen the adaptive strategy of a meditating monk, concentrating resources in a single strip of living bark, a lone spray of needles.

Like the wilderness, the survival of the bristlecones depends on everything we can imagine and much that we cannot. The old trees strike a delicate balance between the exuberance of living and the patience of dying, demanding just enough sustenance and moisture from their mountaintops to live, but in need of no more than the ridgelines can provide. They tolerate drought and winter and minimal reproductive success. They measure growth cell by cell. They live for five thousand years. These ancient and elegant trees symbolize Nevada wilderness.

As for that second illusion, the desert's pervasive sense of wildness may lull even the most passionate advocate into believing that backcountry Nevada is safe from destructive change. Surely, with mountain islands that allow for the longevity of bristlecones, and basins that allow dust storms to play over playas for a hundred miles, the wild heart of Nevada has a safe home. The astutely cynical historian Bernard DeVoto spoke for this illusion fifty years ago when he said of this place, "Not much more can happen. There are plenty of square miles but there are no more water sources. . . . Nevada will remain the least populous state and the one with the widest open spaces. It will be the first Western state to attain a stable equilibrium with the desert."

DeVoto would not mind being wrong. At the beginning of the twenty-first century, Nevada is the fastest-growing state. The atomic blasts of the fifties foreshadowed the human population explosion of the nineties, when Nevada grew by 66 percent. Clark County, encompassing Las Vegas and its surroundings, is the nation's fastest-growing county. Global climate change and introduced species transform the nature of the desert itself.

DeVoto loved a good ironic paradox, and he would mine the surprise of these facts for essays. The citizens of the United States share in the ownership of 83 percent of Nevada, a stunning expanse of public lands. These are the people's wildlands. Large preserves are crucial, here as everywhere. We need continuous habitat for wildlife, multiple variations on pristine desert habitats for science, and large reserves to ensure solitude and awe for human pilgrims. And yet as they begin to lose their isolation, Nevada's Big Empties remain unknown and uncelebrated—prey to the notion that their highest and best use is to store our nuclear waste.

We know that mountain lions and desert bighorn sheep and Lahontan cutthroat trout need wilderness. We humans need wild country as well. Wildlands remain the foundation and framework for our relationship with the earth and its plants and creatures. These arid reaches of basin and range carry fundamental messages about time and quiet and wildness. Dust storms sing, distances speak, aridity teaches.

In these silences and songs and stories we rediscover our context. We resume a conversation with the matrix that shaped us, the wild source of our strength and our peace.

At the Insistence of the Wind—

———————•••⟨∞⟩•••———————

LILACE MELLIN GUIGNARD

Above, a golden eagle follows the line of utility poles out of sight. I leave the tease of the power line's rain-like crackling for silence and a spring vista that, other than the road, is visually unmarked by humans. White bottoms bob away from me, growing smaller among the silver-green sagebrush and yellow-green Mormon tea. I revise my earlier thought. The fleeing pronghorn are clear marks of human impact. Mine.

For once my *Gazetteer* and the USGS map agree that a road running east into the Sage Hen Wash lies before me. In my efforts to map wilderness, I am to follow this road, which links with others, patrolling the perimeter of the Sahwave Mountains, documenting what roads are actually here and what ones aren't. In this way a citizens' inventory is made of areas having wilderness characteristics. Thinking my GPS unit might be a little off, I leave the shade of my GMC pick-up and scan the burled sage carpet for double tracks the way I scanned fields of corn in the southeast, waiting for that moment when my angle was such that the crops miraculously ordered themselves into rows stretching far off. Not today. This is a road that is no longer a road. Pleased, I photograph the nothing that is there, note it on my topo, and head off to circle in the other direction.

What really changes with wilderness designation? Infractions on an individual basis will continue. The Bureau of Land Management gains little, if any, extra funds to help monitor use. And cows will remain—current grazing access is grandfathered into wilderness law. A significant change for Nevada—which is one of the world's largest gold producers— is the restriction on mining. Only valid claims made prior to midnight on December 31, 1983, may be worked in Wilderness Areas. And off-roaders would be told to park their jeeps, trucks, OHVs, and bikes at the boundary road. The arguments over *how* wilderness is used are also arguments over *who* uses wilderness. Many argue that identifying an area as wilderness encourages people who never cared about the area before to come romp all over, that we're better off leaving it unnamed. That Nevada just wants to be left alone.

After spending the night parked in the middle of the road (I was *that sure* no one would come along), I wake to wind gusts shoving dark clouds at Nache Peak's white crest. After granola and orange juice on the tailgate, I'm off again. Every time I climb out of the cab to take a photo or follow tire tracks, the wind assaults me. Sometimes joined by light rain, it pushes against my back, my face, saying *faster, faster.* Descriptions of the desert often emphasize stillness and silence;

but now, instead of feeling calm, I feel impatient. Also blessed. This stormy spring weather brings a quality of light, color, and mood that increases my quality of attention. The scene feels like a rare intimacy, and, though I don't feel I've earned it, I'm glad to deepen my connection with this place. The desert smells especially potent in the drizzle. Wind presses the scent of sage into every pore.

I've attended local meetings where folks—especially members of the sagebrush rebellion that challenges federal authority on public lands—expressed concern that the government and environmentalists want to grab as much land as possible from the public. The land we love and on which we regularly recreate is Nevada land, and given the disrespect Congress has shown it concerning the Yucca Mountain issue, it's no wonder there is deep distrust. But bumping along, trying to dodge blue and white lupine, I think of other fears—fears that corporate industries will succeed in gaining access to these last remote places, lands designated as public but too often consumed by the greedy for the good of the few.

It's naïve anymore to think that Nevada will be left alone. I believe the National Forest Service and the Bureau of Land Management can be Nevada's allies in retaining the character of the tough, open land. Our state pride grew from the challenge of this landscape, and perhaps we can agree on this: Above all, it is the land that makes Nevadans different from

New Yorkers, North Carolinians different from Alaskans. By preserving the land, we preserve our origins, influences, and diversity.

Down at my feet is a rare clumping of bunchgrasses, most of which were run out of town by cheat grass, which became sheriff when humans let cattle overgraze. The grass leans away from the wind, while I fight the urge to walk stooped. Shuffling to the truck, I study the hardy shrubs that came along sometime after the drying of Lake Lahontan in the Pleistocene Era. Then it hits me. What we need is a *real* sagebrush rebellion. If these plants had as much agency as humans, we'd be in for a major attitude adjustment.

Normally, in the breeding season, the male Western meadowlark's song—frenzied, territorial, and glorious—would populate the air. But I hear nothing but the sage being whipped into a sea-green froth. Normally, when I come to the backcountry—for hours, days, or weeks—it's to escape the demands of time. Today the wind howls through what, with luck, we'll have the good sense to designate as wilderness. But we'd better hurry. Time is disappearing, and, unlike bunchgrasses, cannot be reintroduced.

Testimony

UNITED STATES SENATOR
RICHARD BRYAN

I first became captivated by the Black Rock twenty years ago, as governor of Nevada, when I responded to a request by my old college debate coach, Bob Griffin, to join him, his wife, and a few others to camp overnight at the Black Rock. Recalling my days as an undergraduate at the University of Nevada, I knew Bob had an intense interest in the landscapes of Western America. In traveling to debate tournaments by automobile, Bob tried to arouse our interests in the desert country through which we traveled. Those efforts, in my case, were largely unsuccessful.

Members of my staff who were joining us on the encampment urged a more open mind, pointing out the nineteenth-century history of the Black Rock. Indeed, the Black Rock played a significant role in western migration. As the Oregon territory opened up in the 1840s, and later when gold was discovered in California, tens of thousands of pioneers took the Lassen Applegate Trail, which passes through the Black Rock. My interest was piqued, but I was still skeptical of my colleagues who were rhapsodic about the pristine beauty of the Black Rock.

As we drove up to Gerlach and observed the ancient playa that had hosted several major attempts at a land-speed record, I was impressed by its size and how this vastness revealed the curvature of the earth. After taking refreshment during the obligatory stop at Bruno's Country Club in Gerlach, we headed to our campsite to join the rest of our party. As we drove, I noticed that the wet spring had left a fair amount of water, always a welcome sight in the desert.

That evening, Bob and his wife Marguerite began sharing with us stories of hardy pioneers who'd passed through Black Rock—the adversity they faced and the uncertainties that lay ahead for them. That night, as I tossed and turned, listening to the wind, I reflected on how difficult the trip would have been 125 years ago and what courage and perseverance those emigrants who made the passage demonstrated.

As we retraced their travel route the following day, I was struck by the fact that I was seeing what they saw—unspoiled mountain vistas, virtually unchanged in more than a century. I was fascinated when Bob produced sketches of the landscape that J. Goldsborough Bruff, a West Point graduate and topographer, had made during an 1849 trip, which had been forgotten until the end of the nineteenth century. I have no particular navigational aptitude (as a young lieutenant going through army basic training, I had to repeat the compass course), but it was possible for me to identify from Bruff's detailed sketches exactly where he had stood in 1849. As we forged our trail toward High Rock Canyon, the topography became more rugged. While in the canyon we saw, painted in axle grease and still readable, names of some early pioneers and the dates they had passed through.

Nevada, as I knew it as a boy, was rapidly changing. The 110,000 residents of the early 1940s had reached a million and would double in another decade. Having witnessed first-hand how the enormous growth in Southern Nevada had placed extraordinary pressure on the region's natural resources, I feared urban forces would soon have a negative impact on the Black Rock.

A decade later, as a member of the U.S. Senate, I returned to the Black Rock, this time to Soldier Meadows, to learn about its history. Here, John C. Frémont and Kit Carson had camped during their 1843–44 expedition. The trip renewed my interest in preserving what I had been able to see. My hope was to forge a consensus among the conservation community, those who made their living from the public land, such as ranchers and miners, and recreationists, such as off-road racing enthusiasts and hunters. Surely it ought to be possible to provide enhanced protection for the Black Rock without excluding the ranchers and recreationists. The federal government's public land activities have fueled much debate and suspicion in rural Nevada. Many believe that the federal land management agencies harbor an unstated agenda to force the miners and ranchers off public lands. I do not share their suspicion, but I do know that their feelings are strong and are, for some, an article of faith. It is equally difficult to deal with the skepticism of the off-road enthusiasts, hunters, and others who also question the federal land management agencies' motives and view their activities as a thinly disguised effort to close off their access to the public domain.

The conservationists are certain that if no action is taken to provide added protection, the Black Rock in its pristine condition will be lost forever. The gulf between these competing perspectives is too broad to achieve the hoped-for consensus.

As my senate career was coming to a close, my thoughts were of the future. Nevadans of today can see the vistas and relive the emigrant experience, much as our forbearers did 125 years ago, I thought, but what about Nevadans of tomorrow? The births of my grandchildren and my decision not to seek re-election brought a sense of urgency to the cause.

My goal was to preserve the viewscape, the trail, and the wonderful chronicle of the journey of the first emigrants, memorialized in High Rock Canyon—in short, to create an emigrant experience for twenty-first-century Americans to enjoy and relive. I felt that establishing an interpretative center could do much to enhance the visitor experience in future years. I envisioned a place where visitors could retrace the great migration west along the Lassen-Applegate Trail and study artifacts from that era.

I believed all this could be accomplished without prohibiting grazing, hunting, off-road vehicle use, or the annual Burning Man event at the Black Rock. A National Conservation Area, I reasoned, would provide the additional protection needed and the necessary flexibility to continue other public uses.

Nevada's newest Conservation Area became a reality with Congressional approval in the U.S. Senate in 2003. The new NCA status enables the state to compete more effectively for federal funds and makes it possible for all of us to relive the emigrant experience of mid-nineteenth-century America. This fascinating chapter in American history has captured the imagination of the American people.

We can be proud as Nevadans to have preserved a fragile part of our heritage.

The Blank Spot on the Map

UNITED STATES SENATOR
HARRY REID

Encompassing most of the rugged, largely federally managed, arid land of the Great Basin and Mojave Desert between the Sierra Nevada and the Wasatch Range, Nevada is home to the wildest lands remaining in America, outside Alaska. Few Americans, even those well-versed in geography, recognize Nevada as the most mountainous state in the Lower 48. More than 300 mountain ranges grace the Silver State, twenty-six of which are capped by peaks higher than 10,000 feet.

Throughout my life, I have had the opportunity to travel Nevada by plane, car, and foot. The landscape of my home state never ceases to amaze and inspire me. Many of Nevada's mountain ranges show signs of Ice Age glaciers, and some host plant and animal species found nowhere else on Earth. From aspen groves populated by growing elk herds in the Schell Creek Mountains, to the alpine landscape home of mountain goats in the Ruby Mountains, to the secret springs that sustain life for desert bighorn sheep across the Mojave Desert, Nevada's basins and ranges represent the true Wild West and one of America's best-kept secrets.

Though some classic "rock and ice" wilderness exists in Nevada, much of my state's wild country lacks water, much less waterfalls. These are wild lands, but lands that defy conventional conceptions of wilderness. The Jarbidge Mountains near the Idaho border, which were designated by the Wilderness Act of 1964, were the only official wilderness in Nevada until 1989, when—long after all the other western states created their Forest Service wilderness lands—I succeeded in passing a bill designating over 530,000 acres of Forest Service lands throughout the state as wilderness. This bill largely resolved the question of Forest Service wilderness in Nevada but left unanswered which of the Bureau of Land Management's 100+ Wilderness Study Areas merit inclusion in the Federal Wilderness System.

Interestingly, most people view Nevada as a great blank spot on the map, defined by connecting the dots: Las Vegas . . . Death Valley . . . Reno . . . Boise . . . Salt Lake City . . . the Grand Canyon . . . Las Vegas. Sadly, those who advocate Nevada as a place for dumping high-level nuclear waste have a blind spot for the beauty of the blank spot. They choose not to see, or worse yet, to ignore, an inspiring landscape of breathtaking valleys and regal mountains—a diversity of basins and ranges that defies the imagination of those who have never seen it. Although famous for its neon lights and gaming, Nevada is notable also because of its untamed outback; few states can promise a wilderness experience within a half-hour drive from almost anywhere in the state. These are places virtually unchanged since Nevada entered the Union in 1864.

The locations of pioneer efforts in Nevada reflect the ancient concentration of precious metals and the modern distribution of water. Areas throughout Nevada blessed by gold, silver, and copper have at some point or points in time hosted ephemeral mining camps. Those blessed by prodigious springs or flowing creeks provided anchor points for perennial ranches and trading posts. Both water and gold are rare in Nevada (though Nevada ranks third in gold production worldwide, behind South Africa and Australia). Where these resources do not occur, the country remains essentially unsettled.

What remains in Nevada's outback are traces of earlier peoples: petroglyphs etched by American Indians, ghost towns of mining camps long since played out, and desiccated remnants of abandoned ranches. In between are wildlands where outdoor enthusiasts of all descriptions can test their mettle and recharge their souls in the peace, quiet, and solitude of rough country defined and blessed in part by what is not there.

Testimony

STEVEN NIGHTINGALE

You must get your living by loving.
—HENRY DAVID THOREAU

In thy long Paradise of Light . . .
—EMILY DICKINSON

By the age of twenty-four, I had learned much about the attack on other life forms that humans (mostly men) have carried on over the centuries—an attack which, in the spirit of consistency, we have directed with equal viciousness toward each other. Our ability to heal the sick has always been overmatched by our habit of extermination.

The world I saw had turned away from all but human meaning. Any of us could be summed up in social, psychological, political, or economic terms. In our separate human world, life was easy to figure, according to this arithmetic of reality: pleasure, power, income, position, fulfillment. By such measures, you could sum up a man or woman; you could know them.

I could not see my way forward in the society I had been trained—that is, educated—to join. The work of understanding had, in my culture, been mostly set aside in favor of a dark, fierce progress. At the same time, history shows clearly what grows in us, sooner or later, when we are without understanding. Hatred grows, like gangrene.

I was, in so many ways, an intense young idiot. If I have any redemption at all from my idiocy, it is due to my visits, beginning that same year, to the wilderness of the Great Basin. I began in the Black Rock Desert; soon I was hiking every weekend throughout the Great Basin—into the brandy-colored canyons, along the skirts of alkali plains, high up through hidden and glittering aspen; far out in the country with the perfect cougar, golden eagle, horned owl, and graceful bull snake.

The Great Basin has enough land for light—sunlight, starlight, moonlight, morning light, twilight—to show its clarity, playfulness, and suavity. A lustrous world comes forth once again. Light, we are told, comes first in creation. To be simple witness to light is one way to seek communion with this world. By such communion, we can see that when the movement of water makes a canyon, the movement of heaven becomes visible on Earth.

What if, beyond conflict and history, we are meant to understand this comely world? What if we are summoned by the world's beauties? What if we are meant to see things whole, to learn the story and calculus of reality? All things, in such an understanding, would be related precisely and beautifully, and the symposium of the whole would be there for the cherishing. We can know such cherishing in country so generous that, like a lover, it gives all its gifts away, every day, forever.

Are we doomed to suffering and separation? Within the sun, separate hydrogen atoms come together and fuse. That unity makes light. On Earth, we work and play in hopes of just such coming together—of man and woman, body and soul, mind and nature, the rock of the planet and the radiance of language. By such unity, a sentence is made song, belief made knowledge, living made loving, the earth made home.

We need not be condemned to useless learning, like a death in darkness thick as oil. In the Great Basin's bounty of light, anyone can learn what counts, what is useful. How can we know what to do, unless we try to see where the light is going?

The Lexus and the Wilderness Area

CHERYLL GLOTFELTY

In his best-selling book on globalization, *The Lexus and the Olive Tree,* Thomas L. Friedman, a foreign affairs columnist for *The New York Times,* makes a convincing case that the world as we knew it during the Cold War era is over. The Berlin Wall is just one of the walls that have come tumbling down since the late 1980s as the spread of free-market capitalism and the proliferation of communications technology and the Internet have created a global village, where few barriers remain to the worldwide flow of finance, technology, and information. Friedman predicts that it will be possible within a decade to be hooked into a global "Evernet," creating a world in which "we will all be able to be online all the time," no matter where we are. Indeed, our location itself need never be in doubt as Global Positioning Satellites can already pinpoint precisely where we are at all times.

While Friedman believes that globalization is inevitable and is potentially a good thing, he cautions that in this new era of interconnectedness, the challenge—for countries and individuals—will be to maintain a balance between what he calls the Lexus and the Olive Tree. The Lexus, a luxury car made by Toyota, symbolizes the universal human desire for prosperity and an improving standard of living, a desire that is the driving force behind globalization. An equally powerful human value is represented by Friedman's Olive Tree, which stands for people's fierce attachments to particular cultures, communities, nations, and places. Our identity is tied to the local even as we become wired and linked to the global. Thus, Friedman, who surmises that he may have dined at more McDonald's restaurants in more different countries than anyone else in the world, can at the same time profess to be a Minnesotan. Even as the world becomes increasingly homogenized—Big Macs really do taste the same no matter where you buy them, he says—each country needs to develop means of maintaining its cultural and natural distinctiveness; otherwise, globalization will turn cultures into "a global mush" and environments into "a global mash." If countries don't develop sufficiently strong "cultural and environmental filters," he warns, "everywhere will start to look like everywhere else, with the same Taco Bells, KFCs, and Marriotts, with the same malls, MTV and Disney characters, with the same movies, music and Muzak, with the same naked forests and concrete valleys. Touring the world will become like going to the zoo and seeing the same animal in every cage—a stuffed animal."

Wilderness Area designation can be understood in this context as a legal and management "filter" or tool by which the people of the United States can prevent the complete mauling or "malling" of America and can preserve the distinctiveness of particularly special places for themselves and future generations.

Some might argue that globalization and wilderness are inherently at odds and that any attempt to establish Wilderness Areas is therefore a doomed, rearguard action taken by people averse to change, like a child at the beach who builds a wall around his sand castle to protect it from the incoming tide. Only time will tell whether the filter of Wilderness Area designation will be strong enough to stem the tide of development. I think it will, because I think that Wilderness Areas will play an important role in a globalized world, and people will realize that it is in their own best interest to keep them protected. Wilderness Areas will be where we go when we want to be offline, when we want to see real animals, when we want to smell willows along a stream or hear the cascading notes of a rock wren. Whether we are in a high-pressure executive meeting in a skyscraper or are ringing up a cigarette sale in a corner 7-Eleven, we will find comfort in knowing that somewhere "out there" a pygmy nuthatch mother is poking her head into the hole of a pine tree to check on her nestlings. Considered in Friedman's terms, setting aside Wilderness Areas is one way to maintain the important balance between the Olive Tree and the Lexus.

While globalization may pose a threat to Wilderness Areas, it also enables them. In a globalized, post-industrial America,

whose economy is increasingly powered by knowledge industries, such as software design, Internet marketing, commercial banking, insurance, high-end healthcare, biotechnology,
and telecommunications, we won't need every acre of American soil to produce crops or to be converted to steel mills. In
a globalized and ever more urban world, it will be in our economic best interest to establish Wilderness Areas and keep
them wild, as their development would *lower* the value of
these pristine areas as tourist destinations for wilderness
recreationalists. Nevada is a perfect case in point. Nevada has
been the fastest-growing state in the nation for nearly two
decades. Demographically, it is one of the most, if not *the*
most, urban states in America, with its population concen-
trated in the Las Vegas and Reno metropolitan areas. While
the vast expanses of Nevada's hinterland may look mo-
notonously brown from the window of an airplane or uni-
formly barren from the seat of a car, in fact each mountain,
each drainage, each valley, each elevation of this Great Basin
state has a unique character, a marvelous particularity, a distinctive flora and fauna, its own aroma. Volunteers and federal workers have carefully profiled each of Nevada's Wilderness Study Areas, and each one is as quirky, precious, and
irreplaceable as a family member. It may be that all the empty
space that providence put in Nevada in the guise of a "wasteland" was just a crafty way of keeping us from developing
places we would one day need for Wilderness Areas!

Finally, globalization enables wilderness in another way as well. Even as the engines of development threaten to gobble up, pave over, and pollute every corner of the globe, concomitant developments in computer technology and communications make it possible to launch effective campaigns to protect selected areas from these very engines. The Friends of the Nevada Wilderness, for example, have set up a Web site on which anyone in the world can become acquainted with the special character of each of Nevada's Wilderness Areas and Wilderness Study Areas. Check it out for yourself at www. nevadawilderness.org. By clicking on "What You Can Do," anyone in the world can participate in protecting these places. Roberta Moore used e-mail to solicit submissions to this volume, and I used Microsoft Word on my iMac to compose this essay, which I then zapped to Moore electronically as an attachment file. The fundamental question posed by globalization was framed by Henry David Thoreau 150 years ago. Do we control our machines or do they control us? If we harness the tools of globalization to preserve what we value—to create "livability" for ourselves and future generations—then we have reason to welcome these new machines. On the other hand, if we stand impotent as the machines of globalism destroy what we love, then these machines control us. I say, let's grab the wheel, drive the Lexus to the Wilderness Area, and reconnect with our Olive Tree—or, in Nevada, our Piñon Pine.

Yucca Mountain Wilderness

REBECCA MILLS

Wild, backcountry, woods, wastelands—look up "wilderness" in your computer's thesaurus, and these are the alternative words you are likely to find.

Look up "wasteland," and the thesaurus suggests words such as *desert, solitude, waste, sand, wilderness.*

Is Yucca Mountain—not the mountain, but the planned nuclear-waste depository—just a cultural oxymoron, the manifestation of century-old thinking still present in powerful minds? It's in the desert. It's a place of solitude. It's certainly backcountry. The thesaurus mirrors our confusion. More certainly, Nevada is a state with few people and relatively little political power; and we have known for decades that human-waste products get located in such places. Since the president, the Department of Energy, and the majority in Congress consider Yucca Mountain a wasteland, and the thesaurus suggests the alternative "wilderness," what does this tell us about ourselves?

How many American citizens still drive through Nevada seeing "waste" in the sea of sagebrush and waves of mountain ranges instead of brilliantly diverse ecosystems evolved over millennia to survive in a tough climate? How long have we known that there is no true "wasteland" in nature, that the earth has evolved effective recycling and waste-treatment facilities? How long before enough of us evolve to understand the implications of producing radioactive waste with a half-life so long-lived that we can barely comprehend it? When will we realize we should not produce something we do not know how to manage safely?

Is it too late for Yucca Mountain? Is it too late to protect the lands downwind from the highways along which waste will be trucked to Yucca Mountain? Accidents will happen. Is it too late to protect the drinking water of nearby towns, water interconnected with the aquifer underlying Yucca Mountain? Read the Environmental Impact Statement for Yucca Mountain, and see if it convinces you that people—let alone the natural world—will be protected.

It is not too late. It will be years before the facility is ready to accept the high-level radioactive waste. Nevada's people and political representatives are fighting. The Washington, D.C., Circuit Court of Appeals agrees that the project is not safe. More science is needed. Yucca Mountain is a wilderness. Think about it.

Nevada No Longer

SHAUN GRIFFIN

> This is a case in which the public
> has to trust the scientists.
> —TONY BUONO, USGS Hydrologist,
> Nevada Test Site

Nevada is never on the map, not now,
not ever.
      If only
I could finger a word
for the few who live
          by the sun,
what would it be: itinerant,
sparse dragon people
          who fly
in the sand and spin before the books
that name a cactus to clothe
the loins of uranium down deep?

No, it would not be harsh; rather
we live here.

Nevada No Longer

We raise family, split wood,
shovel snow, and read of our absence.

Nevada is never on the map,
not now, not ever,
          save the day
a green lung percolates
from two miles below volcanic tuff—
then you will recognize us
as the place that kills
or was killed, but for now
I cannot find a way down Alternate 95—
not scholarly, not radical, not
known. And still, faces cling
to the taverns of Beatty,
Tonopah, and Yerington.

Where do I go to lie with the yucca? California?
No, it is many things but quiet.
Oregon? No, it is wet and
dry there, so I remain
home
with states before and aft
coming like insects
to the Test Site, coming
with something to read.

Today, I tell my son
of a desert with no name. He remarks
"Why?" I do not know—Nevada is
never on the map, not now,
not ever.

From *Bathing in the River of Ashes* (Reno: University
of Nevada Press, 1999).

A Gesture of Faith and Forgiveness

TERRY TEMPEST WILLIAMS

There are two kinds of wilderness in Nevada. The first is a wilderness of ecological integrity that is unagitated and free. The second is a wilderness of waste, dangerous and desolate. One cannot honor and protect the first wilderness without acknowledging the sorrow of the second.

I have walked both wildernesses in the state of Nevada. One made my heart sing, the other made my body weep. I am talking about the atomic wilderness of the Nevada Test Site and the condemnation of Yucca Mountain to hold what makes human hands shrivel, the blistering death sentence carried by the weight of this nation's nuclear waste.

What I want to say is simply this: With my boot holding down the lower barbed wire and slowly slipping under the one above without getting cut, I quietly entered the Nevada Test Site. Never will I forget walking for hours undetected in the Joshua tree forest toward Mercury. I had in my backpack an old bulletin, a volume of *The Great Basin Naturalist* published in the 1960s, that listed birds found dead on these poisoned lands after nuclear bombs had been tested. Mourning doves, bluebirds, horned larks, black phoebes, and spotted sandpipers were among the corpses found. Each step taken across the Mojave Desert became more terrifying than the next. This land bears scars in its stretched skin, a physical record of each explosion born in illuminated horror. If a landscape can look beaten, battered, and abused, this land did. Strange algae, blue-green, covered white rocks. Was that a lizard with two tails? Of course, I could have fallen prey to my own imagination. But my mother was dead, my grandmothers were dead, buried alongside aunts—all women who belonged to the Clan of One-Breasted Women, women in my family who died of cancer. Nuclear Fallout: Our future was carried out by the wind. I walked these desert lands in violation of the law to honor them. I wanted to believe and participate in a higher law—not as a trespasser, but as a participant. I wanted to walk as far as I could before being arrested and to leave offerings of peace in a land that had been stolen for war.

True wilderness is a refuge of peace.

Nevada, with her history of sacrifice in the name of war, should now be given her due for the high price paid in our nation's nuclear history. If there is a healing to occur, let it be in her wildlands of the first order. May we protect them, preserve them, cherish them. May this act of wilderness designation, proposed by citizens and granted by Congress, become a gesture of faith and forgiveness for the lands we have killed, a graceful compensation for the nuclear wilderness that can never be restored except through our memories of remorse and respect.

Nuclear Destruction of Shoshone Land

CORBIN HARNEY

The land that became the Nevada Test Site was very important for us native people because that's where we roamed through back and forth, going south to the warm country during the winter months and going north when it was warmer. We moved according to the seasons to find our foods; down south they grow earlier in the year—certain kinds of seeds, certain kinds of roots. It was important to us because we were told by our forefathers, "Make sure you take care of your food; take care of what you survive on."

Those are the reasons we were concerned when President Truman set aside land for the Nevada Test Site, telling the world it was for military use, to protect the United States and the people. This is what we were told, but actually the United States government didn't come to us and ask us if they could use it. They claimed they had made a treaty with the Shoshone people that said they were going to protect our land, protect our rights. The story can go on and on and on, but I'm only going to talk a little bit about it. We, as native people in this part of the country, in this part of the continent, protect the land—our Mother Earth, as we call it—because we suck from it, we get our food from it. The Nevada Test Site was very important for my people because they passed through there and they lived back there, seventeen miles from the town of Mercury, where the workers from the nuclear energy department stay. The government now says those workers are the ones who control this place. My people used to live back there where the springs and the pine-nut trees were, where a lot of sunflowers grew. Our people talked about how important this place was because it provided plenty of food, plenty of animal life—deer, antelope, lots of things we survived on.

Those are the reasons why the native people took care of that land. "You have to take care of all the living things," we were told from the beginning of our lives. Different kinds of plants have different kinds of seeds; different berries, different purposes. Some plant life is used for medicine. So we were concerned after we found out that President Truman set that land aside for military use and they started testing bombs, all different kinds of bombs. We were concerned because it was going to destroy the life in that place, life that was put there by the nature—whether the life crawls, whether the life flies, whether it walks, whatever it does. We survive off that land, which had a lot of bigger pine nuts. That's why my people lived there for many years.

When the government set that land aside for military use, they moved the native people elsewhere and told us, "We are going to move you. We are going to set some land aside for you." We didn't understand. Why were they going to set our own land aside for us? They said the government had made a treaty with the Shoshone people in October 1863. I don't think the native people made any agreement; I think they were told to sign it, told it was going to protect their land—26 million acres of land where they could hunt, gather their berries, pine nuts, seeds of all different kinds.

We have always been very concerned about bird life, animal life of all different kinds, and the water we drank. So we got upset about the Test Site because we knew testing bombs was going to take life, all kinds of life. So far that's what the testing has done and that's what it will continue to do, which is why we don't appreciate what our government is doing to the world. We thought the United States government was supposed to protect the lives of all different creatures on this part of the earth. They always say, "You have to protect human life, be concerned about life of all kinds." So far what we've seen is not what they said they were going to do. It was awful to find out later that this land had been set aside by the government for military use—to find out what damage a bomb developed at the Test Site could do to the human race, how many human lives throughout the world it could take. We asked the federal government, "Why are you taking so many lives? For what reason?"

This is something we're still concerned about today. Remember, the United States government had a war going on when the Test Site was established, and they wanted to develop a bomb to drop on another country. That's what they did. Does our government realize how many lives they were taking then and are still taking today? Are they glad to be thinning the people out? Look what our government has done to Japan, to their people, their land, their water. Today it still goes on. The nuclear bomb is going to take lives and continue to take lives. We weren't told that this bomb is going to destroy this world of ours, but we have witnessed that life has been taken, that living things on this Mother Earth of ours—plant life, animal life, bird life, creatures that crawl—have been crippled. Things that we lived on for thousands and thousands of years are disappearing. For generations we took care of our Mother and our Mother had supported us, fed us, gave us plenty of water, good air. Today, with the nuclear bomb, we seem to be trying to get rid of what we need for survival. We're concerned about developing bombs to destroy the world.

It should never have been that way. If the government had come out and talked to us as native people, they would have found out from the very beginning that we don't own the land; everything on this Mother Earth owns it together; the plant life owns it, animals own it, the creatures that crawl own it. We're all caretakers—or we're supposed to be, as humans. We're the ones who are supposed to have ceremonies. We had our ceremonies at the Test Site for many years before the Europeans came to this part of the continent because that was a very important place. During the winter months, we roamed there where the animals gather. Everything used to be clean there, and since the Test Site started in 1948, little by little we have begun to miss a lot of things that were put there for us as people. We want our young people to enjoy looking at the land as the years go on. Now they have fences around the land that say "Keep out."

We say we're concerned about our children, that we're concerned about the lives of different kinds of animals and birds. Seems to me the government doesn't care so I hope people can wake up and start thinking about these things. What are you going to tell your children, your grandchildren? If the beautiful land, beautiful animals of all different kinds are gone from the face of this Mother Earth, are we going to say we didn't care for them, that we did something wrong?

So this is why I'm saying something about this now. In the Ruby Valley Treaty of 1863 that was ratified by Congress in 1869, the government said they were going to take care of us. Maybe they forgot what they said: They would hold this land in trust for us, protect our hunting rights, our fishing rights.

"We are going to take care of the land. We're going to take care of you," is what they told us. Sounded really good then, but where is it now? I hope the people around the world realize the truth about the treaty the United States government made with the native people, telling us, "We're going to give you money for the damage that we have done to the land." Some of the native people took that money.

How long is this Mother Earth going to provide us with life if we continue to put poison on it? This radiation is poison. So many people have lost their lives since we developed the nuclear bomb and nuclear energy.

When Yucca Mountain was set aside, the government never told the world that they were going to put waste from nuclear power plants from throughout the country into that mountain. That's another concern of ours because if you look at Yucca Mountain from the south to the north—my people from generation to generation have talked about this—there is a snake in that mountain going north. Those small rolling hills have movement in them. We, the native people, tried to tell the nuclear energy department that the mountain moves. They didn't believe what we were saying because their scientists and engineers get good money from the nuclear energy department. All they are concerned about is money. Their leaders keep saying to them that this is native land. The federal government controls it because the federal government has said from the beginning that they were going to take care of the native people's land under trust. So this is something that we witness ourselves. The nuclear energy department started drilling tunnels in the hill. They are going to put nuclear waste in it.

What does it mean to that hill when you put a radiation poison in it, right next to seven volcanoes that were alive there not too long ago? Right in an earthquake zone that still moves today, and will move tomorrow. Our people said the snake moves a little at a time. I think the scientists realize this, but they don't want to talk about it to the world because they're making good money. We also know, as native people, that there's a caliche line between the top and the foot of this rolling hill. That caliche is made of clay that we used to cover our houses. The scientists thought the tunnel was going to hold water, but it leaks today because of the earthquakes. There are holes in that clay that hold water—all clay has holes in it. We are concerned about it because if you put a few thousand rods together in that tunnel, how hot is that moisture from the leaking water going to get? That's what puts steam out from the nuclear rods. Yet they're telling us they're going to put 77,000 tons of waste in this tunnel, nuclear waste from all over the country. How safe is it going to be? If an earthquake cracks this caliche, more and water will get into the nuclear rods, and it's going to get hot. Are we trying to blow this part of the country up? If it does explode, what chance do we, the human race, have on this Mother Earth?

We have already seen what happens when they put nuclear bombs in the earth: It destroys our water table. Our scientists are not telling us those things, but they are putting signs out there: "Do not drink this water."

We have already taken many lives with nuclear power. From the beginning of the nuclear bomb, how many lives have been taken? People throughout the world have suffered from it, but we have continued to develop those dangerous things. It's sad to see our government become murderers all over this world. I don't know how many people are going to be left if an accident happens. We all are going to suffer because we have seen so many people dying today because of cancer caused by nuclear power. We have to do something about nuclear power because it's making our Mother sick. We're all going to be affected by these things. Our air is not clean, we can't drink the water, the animal life is getting thinner and thinner, and soon we won't have any food. If you don't think about it, then the nature itself is going to make you think about it.

Gated Mountains

SCOTT SLOVIC

In July 2002, having spent the better part of a Saturday in the office catching up on paperwork, I decided to treat myself, as I routinely do, to a taste of Nevada wilderness. I'm not talking about an impromptu jaunt to one of the state's remote mountain ranges. I'm talking about proximate wilderness, about the possibility of hiking through sage, bitterbrush, mountain mahogany, Jeffrey pines, and multicolored rock, serenaded by the sound of mountain water, just fifteen minutes from downtown Reno.

Tired of my sunless office, eager for the bracing smell of the mountains, I raced home to pick up my wife and our dogs. Susie had been thinking about a walk somewhere in the direction of Mt. Rose—perhaps the Thomas Creek area. But I had in mind another familiar hiking area, a place where I've often walked with my graduate students from the University of Nevada's Literature and Environment Program. I pictured the striking ochre and gray cliffs of Hunter Creek Canyon, the many shades of green tracing the route of the creek from the Mt. Rose Wilderness Area down to the Truckee River.

I arrived in Reno in 1995 to teach in UNR's English Department. A primary attraction of the move was the opportunity to live near mountains, to live *in* the mountains. I had been working for several years in the Texas Hill Country, just southwest of Austin, and was starved for genuine alpine climate and vistas. It didn't take long to discover the popular Steamboat Ditch Trail and the Hunter Creek Trail, both of which were accessed via an informal parking lot in the new Juniper Ridge housing development just south of the Truckee River, two or three miles west of Virginia Street in downtown Reno. Both trails had obviously been used by Reno hikers and runners for years, and the Steamboat Ditch Trail was a favorite location for mountain bikers as well.

But almost immediately it was clear that trail access would be a serious issue in Juniper Ridge, as McMansion after McMansion cropped up on the west-facing ridge. This is nothing new in Reno. All over the city, access to spectacular wild places is threatened by metastasizing urban sprawl. There's Hidden Valley State Park on the eastern side of the city, Peavine Mountain to the north (just a few minutes from the UNR campus), Galena Park and Thomas Creek and Whites Creek to the south, and Steamboat Ditch/Hunter Creek to the west. Wise urban planning would preserve public access to these beautiful areas, much as Boulder, Colorado, has created Chautauqua Park in the nearby Rocky Mountain foothills. The public parks remain open; but, increasingly, Reno's traditional places of outdoor recreation, including the Hunter Creek and Hunter Lake Trails, are on the verge of inaccessibility. They are becoming private viewsheds for wealthy new arrivals.

So the Saturday afternoon hike on Hunter Creek Trail in July 2002 would be a kind of experiment. Susie and I, and my son Jacinto, had recently returned from spending a sabbatical semester in Brisbane, Australia. In addition to our daily urban regimen in Australia, we'd traveled much of the eastern and central regions of that vast country, hiking both rugged and highly engineered trails, dodging lightning on Mt. Kosciuszko in the Snowy Mountains of New South Wales and shivering in the foggy highlands of Tasmania's Cradle Mountain.

We'd been impressed by the enlightened efforts of Australia's state and national governments to create parks and promote public access to wild places and, at the same time, to set aside many pristine wild areas as trail-less habitat for the country's extraordinarily diverse plants and animals. In some ways, our outdoor experiences in Australia reminded Susie of her native Colorado, including the maintenance of lovely trails in the Front Range near Denver and the Flatirons in Boulder. Even in Brisbane, a metropolis of more than a million people, it was possible to leave behind the city noises and scenes on Mt. Coot-tha or in the more distant parts of the Brisbane Forest Park or on nearby North Stradbroke Island and Moreton Island. Wandering around Australia, I often found myself thinking of my hometown of Eugene, Oregon, and the many trails for hiking, running, and biking in the

Cascades just to the east. Like many people, I tend to hold my favorite childhood places as a kind of fixed standard of beauty and joy, thinking, "This is what the world should be like."

I chose Hunter Creek Trail as an experiment in "urban wilderness trail access," knowing as we began the short drive from our house to the trailhead that our experiment would be complete even before we stepped out of the car to begin walking—and knowing, too, that it was likely the results would not be pleasant.

We drove west along the south side of the Truckee River and after a few minutes turned left past the faux gate at the entrance to Juniper Ridge. Up the hill a bit further, and then a right turn onto a street named "Mountaingate." I hadn't noticed this name before, but it seemed ominously appropriate. For several years I've been tracking the progress of the extraordinarily ugly and pretentious mansions of the nouveau riche up this ridgeline, facing the Steamboat Ditch to the west and Hunter Creek Canyon and Mt. Rose Wilderness Area to the south. Rocky lots, scattered with cheat grass and sagebrush, were being replaced, one by one, by bloated stucco castles and greener grass than could be found in nature.

Sure enough, when we arrived at what had served as a public parking area for the past seven years (and probably longer), there was no empty lot. During the past six months, yet another castle had been erected, a monument to the privatization of wilderness access in the American West. The gating of Mt. Rose Wilderness Area, at least from this popular access point, was now almost complete. We drove down the block and found a surreptitious route between two mansions, slipped through with the dogs, and made our way to the Hunter Creek Trail. But we felt as if we were doing something illegal, trespassing in order to get to public land. At the same time, our simple walk felt like an act of necessary defiance. It was a warm July afternoon, and I felt my blood boiling as we hiked. I thought of the man I had seen standing on his greener-than-green "mountaingate" lawn when we drove by, his arms proudly crossed, watching his dog take a shit. His stance seemed to say, "I own this place, this grass, this dog, this shit, this entire valley. I own the Hunter Creek view. No riffraff allowed." I wanted to say to him, "Up yours!" And I wanted to say the same thing to the civic leaders who had allowed Reno, and still allow Reno, to be sold out to distant developers (often located in California and the Midwest, according to scuttlebutt) who have no concern for the beauty and livability of this place, only for the money that can be extracted from it.

...

As a scholar of environmental literature, I know the many historical and philosophical views of wilderness that have percolated in both public and academic circles during recent years and for many decades, even centuries. My bookshelves at home and at work are loaded down with such statements.

Every morning when I look at distant Mt. Rose from my bedroom window and when I kick up the dust on any mountain trail in Reno or elsewhere, I think of Wallace Stegner's elegant proposal, from his so-called "Wilderness Letter" of the early 1960s, that wilderness is the "geography of hope."

I think, too, of Edward Abbey's provocative claim, from *Desert Solitaire,* that we need wilderness even if we never go there (or never can go there); for its mere existence, or the thought of it, gives us a form of refuge from our right-angled, man-made environments. I remember supporting Abbey's claim years ago, as a graduate student in New England, when the memory of wild places in the West helped to sustain me as I wrote my dissertation in stuffy offices on the Brown campus. Western wilderness, the idea of it, filled my dreams and inspired my pen.

And then I moved to Nevada in 1995, just as William Cronon was publishing "The Trouble with Wilderness" in venues suitable for academics (*Uncommon Ground: Toward Reinventing Nature*) and for the general public (*The New York Times*). Cronon's work problematized the concept of wilderness, revealed its social-constructedness and artificiality, and made it easier for developers and road-builders and loggers and miners to buy (or rent at bargain-basement prices) and despoil land that has not for a long time been what "romantic idealists" call "wilderness." While Cronon's ideas may have intellectual merit, they are also a practical fiasco because they seem to provide academic legitimacy to those who wish to log, mine, or graze anywhere they please. Sometimes it's simply best for academics to stay in their offices and chatter to each other.

As I walked the Hunter Creek Trail on that July day in 2002, blood boiling, I found myself remembering Robert Michael Pyle's phrase "the extinction of experience" from his book *The Thunder Tree,* published in 1993. Remembering the High Line Canal from the Aurora, Colorado, of his childhood, Pyle eloquently argues that we are increasingly removed from the more-than-human world in our daily experience of urban America. He argues that many routes to self-understanding and ecological awareness are traveled not by abstract thinking, but by ordinary, daily experience, by using our senses to see, smell, hear, and touch the world. We need urban wildlands, says Pyle, in order to have access to the experience of the world and in order to appreciate who we are and what's important in our lives. The "extinction" of wild experience, even the moderate forms of wild experience that one can have in a city park or a nearby mountain trail, is a significant crisis of our time.

As a scholar/teacher, I, like many people in my city, spend much of my time indoors. Even though I often talk about nature with students and colleagues, we tend to conduct our discussions in built environments, referring abstractly to the world beyond our making. But I also love being outside, and I seek access to the world wherever I can find it. I am not content merely to look at the world from a glorious distance. Although I occasionally find time to wander the Ruby Mountains or the more remote reaches of the Sierra Nevada range, I have always felt that access to the Reno area's small wildernesses is a special blessing of living in this place. As this access frays and vanishes due to the greed of corporate developers and the short-sightedness of city planners and officials (and perhaps even the local electorate), I brood over our collective "extinction of experience."

Here in Nevada we have another "gated mountain" to make our blood boil and to threaten us with "extinction of experience" in an even more literal sense. If people throughout the U.S. know nothing else about Nevada, most have heard of "Yucca Mountain," a place that, according to the Bush Jr. administration, will solve the nation's energy worries by storing 77,000 tons of high-level radioactive waste and enabling nuclear power plants to continue operating and producing more waste ad infinitum. If Yucca Mountain were located in just about any other American state, it would be recognized as a beautiful place, even a sacred place. Because it's located in a state with more than 300 mountain ranges, and because it's located on the Nevada Test Site (part of the federal land that constitutes more than 80 percent of Nevada), it's relatively easy for a White House with its hands in the pockets of the nuclear industry to run a farce of a review process, launch a national publicity campaign loaded with logical and scientific and ethical fallacies, and ram approval of the nuclear-waste repository through Congress. Who will ever know the difference? How many people will ever see firsthand the beauty of this mesa-like topography? How many people know about the twenty species of reptiles that live there?

Yucca Mountain is now a secretive place located 100 miles north of Las Vegas on gated, Test Site land. Just as wilderness areas in the Reno vicinity are increasingly inaccessible to recreational visitors, Yucca Mountain and other military locales in the state are places where the federal government does things it doesn't want scrutinized by the public. For the current federal administration, Yucca Mountain signifies a safe, politically expedient solution to the nuclear waste conundrum. To citizens of Nevada, Yucca Mountain signifies the culmination of a greedy, shortsighted, and scientifically uninformed (or incomplete) energy industry, working in cahoots with a corrupt, self-serving administration. Increasingly, if the predicted waste-transportation accidents do occur, citizens throughout the nation will come to share the critical perspectives of Nevadans—and they'll remember that it was the Bush-Cheney government that stamped its approval on this repository site. Rebecca Solnit wrote in an August 2002 editorial that "the bumpers of the trucks that will carry tens of thousands of loads of nuclear waste to Yucca Mountain should read, 'We're gambling with the inheritance of our children and grandchildren and countless generations after them.'" Yucca Mountain is a "gated" Nevada mountain that gives new meaning to our reputation as a gambling state.

I watch a covey of California quail, a few grown-ups and a brood of nervous chicks, gather seeds from my backyard. We can wait for nature to come to us, and we can view the world from behind glass. Or we can organize ourselves, as individuals and as communities, to speak out for access, for the opportunity to experience our place in the world, and for a responsive, responsible government that does not perceive wilderness, particularly desert, as "a good place to throw used razor blades," in the words of an Atomic Energy Commission official quoted in Terry Tempest Williams's *Refuge*.

· · ·

Should we be content with mountaingate mansions blocking access to proximate wilderness in Reno, in Nevada, in the American West? Are we powerless to act for preservation of trail access in our part of the world? Should we allow Nevada's wild mountains to become synonymous with "nuclear waste"? We should ask ourselves these questions. And we should let our elected officials, and our mountaingate neighbors, know that the public needs and demands access to nearby wild places, to the world's beauty. And that we'd prefer not to have our mountains hollowed out and filled with radioactive garbage.

On the Front Lines

COREY LEE LEWIS

I am standing in the shade of a sandstone cliff, trying to interpret a panel of pictographs that beckons to me across a chasm of time. As the pattern of colored shapes materializes before me, I attempt to trace their faint outlines with my eye, drawing distinctions between rock and pigment—nature and culture—distinctions that have begun to weather and blur over the ages. My eyes sweep across the smooth sandstone wall and leap through the hot Mojave air, eastward toward another vague series of shapes and outlines. Slowly a distinct pattern emerges. Blurred by shimmering heat waves and smog, a jagged city skyline rises out of the desert heat toward the azure sky. I recognize the outlines of the Stratosphere's needle, the Excalibur's castle, and the Luxor's pyramid; and while I can't interpret the pictographic text on the rock next to me, the larger context of the situation is easy to read. I am standing on the front lines of battle, amidst the clash of two cultures, witness to the eradication of history and biodiversity.

Between the four-lane highway ringing the Vegas sprawl and the edge of this proposed Wilderness Area lies a wounded landscape studded with burnt Joshua trees, broken beer bottles, and shot-up appliances, the city's refuse regurgitated upon an innocent land. Soon this landscape of nighttime bon-fires and drunken gunplay will become a monument to a different kind of hedonism as a new subdivision is built in the desert, complete with thirsty golf courses and air-conditioned houses. And yet, at the edge of this urban waste—less than a few minutes' drive in a fossil-fuel-dependent automobile, or a few hours' walk in a pair of hand-woven yucca-fiber sandals from the neon-laced glow of the Las Vegas strip—lies an ancient wilderness with the power to transport visitors back in time.

Brownstone Basin, as it is called today, lies on the eastern-most edge of the Red Rock National Conservation Area, hiding quietly behind a locked gate, and waiting patiently for the protection that will come with wilderness designation. I have come here today with Friends of Nevada Wilderness, Nevada's oldest wilderness advocacy organization. We spent the preceding day, as we often do, huddled under the stale glow of fluorescent lights, conducting the tiresome work of trying to run a wilderness campaign and manage a non-profit organization, and have come here to see one of the places we are fighting to protect. The group spans several generations of people, from veterans like Marge Sill, affectionately dubbed "the Mother of Nevada Wilderness" because she has been defending it since 1959, all the way to new soldiers such as sixteen-year-old Cynthia Scholl, who spends most of her free time volunteering for the organization. Together, we have come to explore these canyons and see what gifts they might have to offer, as well as to confirm our convictions and steel ourselves for the battle over the future of this place, and many others like it, which hangs precariously in the balance.

As we hike into the basin, we are awed by the layers of pink, red, and tan sandstone that form the Calico Hills, a group of petrified sand dunes burning silently in the sun. A series of grayish-brown limestone cliffs rises above these brightly colored formations, giving this basin its current name. The limestone is much older than the Aztec sandstone upon which it rests, a unique reversal of geology known as an "overthrust fault." This particular formation—the Keystone Thrust Fault —is the best example of an overthrust fault in the United States, and perhaps even in the world.

Below these vaulted formations, in the sandy soil of the basin, we find large mounds of chalky white limestone, remnants of agave roasting pits used by the Paiute to cook everything from agave, yucca, and cactus to rabbit, tortoise, and bighorn. When they were used, the heat from these ancient cook pits converted the limestone to calcium hydroxide, turning it an uncharacteristic, chalky white color, and making these important archeological sites easy to find. Like the fragile pictographs painted on the canyon walls, the cook pits are often vandalized and destroyed by those who come here with no knowledge of space or time, with no sense of the sacred.

Millions of years of evolution have been written on these

canyon walls, inscribed in the flowering of an agave, and displayed in the sure-footedness of a bighorn sheep. In the few cryptic traces left by those who once lived here—the Paiute, Shoshone, Anasazi, and others—we can read the wisdom of people who knew the virtue of restraint, who could write their names on the land in language that would not mar it for others, people who knew how to hold places in trust for their children. What kind of legacy will we leave, I wonder, for those who come here after we depart? What Earth will our children meekly inherit? Outside of the proposed Wilderness Area, I find used toilet paper and diapers, broken beer bottles and gun shells, tire tracks and torched Joshua trees, the senseless slaughter of a land once filled with life and bathed in beauty.

My thoughts are drawn back to the horned lizard I almost stepped on while hiking earlier in the day. Despite his squat, tan body and tiny legs, he scampered with surprising dexterity as my foot descended, taking him out of harm's way and into the cover of a nearby sagebrush. I recalled reading that, when threatened, these courageous little reptiles burrow into the sand backwards and shoot a stream of blood directly out of their eyes at their attackers in a desperate attempt to defend their lives and homes.

With the confused skyline of Vegas before me, and my back to the sandstone walls of Brownstone Basin, I wonder if our blood will prove thick enough. I wonder if we have the courage and wisdom it will take to defend this place. As the city recedes from my view, I can only hope that help will come and that others will join our fight before it's too late, before this place and all that lives here are gone forever, before no wild Earth is left for our children to inherit.

Driving With the Enemy

K. ALDEN PETERSON

Late October

6:30 AM

The sun rises with the fierceness of summer. I pull the visor down as the car climbs out of the Truckee River Canyon and up onto Darwin Pass. "The study of geology can drive you mad," I say. Brian says "Hummph." Steinbeck traveled with his dog Charley, who said "Ftt"; I travel with Brian, who says "Hummph." Perhaps for Brian, a prospecting geologist, the study of geology does not lead to madness. If he applies his craft well and figures out the puzzle correctly, he wins. Maybe the study of geology is only madness for me. In college I considered my studies of the earth to be sacred knowledge. My last semester I realized the expectations imparted with a geology degree included dismantling ecosystems and extracting resources. I walked away from my classes and left my geology degree forever dangling. Madness.

Interstate 80, a cement plant, a truck-stop/casino, and the endless structure of the Amazon.com warehouse define Darwin Pass. In the past and again in the future, when Earth's shifting axis brings consistently wetter and cooler climates,

Darwin Pass becomes the location where Pyramid Lake spills over into the Carson Desert. When I look at Darwin Pass, I see water—lines of ancient shorelines ringing mountains to the north, south, and east—and empty channels like finger tracings in sand. To look into the desert and see only water, to see things I will never witness, things older than memory—this too must be madness.

7:10 AM

"The coloration up there is alteration." Brian talks excitedly about time periods spanning 100 million years as he points out features north of the highway. He speaks of entire mountains folded over onto their sides and of hot water solutions bringing gold to the surface during a time of continental collision.

"The Jessup mine is just beyond that hill—very rich," Brian comments. I know about Jessup, too. Up on the ridge, nearly 300 feet above the highway in the gravelly alluvium just below the highest peaks, I see the shoreline of ancient Lake Lahontan. At Lake Lahontan's highest water level, Jessup Embayment was subject to direct assault by storm waves driven over sixty miles of open water. The action of these waves built gravel bars and spits, completely indifferent to the gold.

Several years ago a geologist used a backhoe to cut an inspection trench through one of the highest Jessup Embayment gravel bars. At the bottom of his exposed profile, where rain-washed sediments buried the old high-water beach gravel

[137]

after the lake declined, the geologist discovered the foot bones of a camel. These bones provided an age for the high stand of Lake Lahontan—13,060 years ago. Although I admire knowledge, I've also seen the backhoe trench. The trench endures and will continue to endure until Lake Lahontan again returns. The study of geology has driven me just mad enough to question whether or not certainty in knowing is equal to the destruction of the feature to find out. But, because I left my geology degree dangling, neither my thesis nor my income depends on certainty.

8:15 AM

"That's the Florida Canyon Mine—two million ounces of gold from low-grade ore." Brian points to an artificial mountain partially obscuring a hollowed-out canyon. Low-grade ore— the words terrify me. To extract a single ounce of gold from low-grade ore requires the processing of as much as two hundred tons of rock. Mountains must be disassembled, transported, piled onto leach pads, and sprayed with cyanide.

"They've done a great job of reclamation." The reclamation Brian speaks of involves removing the sharp edges of the leach heaps with bulldozers and planting the resulting "hill" in with crested wheatgrass, rabbitbrush, and sagebrush. What remains is not quite a mountain sitting on a buried rubber pad where a mountain never was before. And the naked canyon beyond shows terraced rock walls that truncate the Humboldt

[138]

Mountains like an amputation scar. Brian admires the work of mining reclamation, but he fears the costs involved will chase mining out of Nevada.

"Good riddance," I say.

Brian accepts this philosophically. "If that's what people want, that's what they are going to get. But when the money from mining stops rolling into the state coffers, then we'll see what they really want."

Is Brian the enemy? Brian represents the latest incarnation of the Cartesian belief system—the system that first pronounced animals soulless in order to rationalize vivisection for the advancement of human understanding. I don't want to sell Brian short; he fought alongside environmental activists for wilderness. For Brian, however, wilderness is an insignificant subset of an inanimate planet surface composed primarily of hidden resources destined for human extraction.

I see the world differently. I do not believe that simply because the rocks, soils, mountains, deserts, rivers, and lakes live at time scales incompressible to humans, they are any less alive than the animal and plant components of Earth. I look upon a strip-mined mountain or a graded and paved desert with the same pangs of empathy I feel when I look at a coyote dragging a mangled leg, the result of an encounter with a steel-spring trap. There is no profit in thinking this way. To embrace such thoughts—madness.

Brian points out the gold mines along the eastern edge of the Osgood Mountains—Preble, Pinson, Getchell, and Chimney Creek. "An extremely rich system of mineralization trends right through here, running north to south." I look beyond the mines to the striking contrast of desert mountains wrapped in the reddish hues of late autumn against the cerulean blue sky of approaching winter.

"I wonder how different this place would be today if the human gene contained a conservation ethic?" I say. "What would Nevada look like if all the humans believed resource use should stop well before animals, plants, mountains, and deserts began dying—before ecosystems collapsed?" The poet Jeffers dreamt of a world where people were fewer and hawks more numerous. I see Jeffers's world every time I look at Earth through the lens of geologic time. Emigrant Canyon, where the toe of the Osgood Mountains dips into the Humboldt River, marks the eastern extent of Lake Lahontan. If humans had not been so human, today there would be horses, camels, mammoths, shrub oxen, Harlan's ground sloths, large-headed llamas, and mastodons feeding in and around the marshes while sabertooth cats, lions, and dire wolves prowled the perimeter.

"If people did not extract resources, there would be no metal," Brian says. "No metal; no cars. We wouldn't be here."

"I would."

"Hummph," Brian says.

"Ftt," I answer.

Brian thinks I am the enemy. One geology degree dangles; the other remains intact. Perhaps the study of geology has driven us both mad.

The Effects of Wilderness Designation—
One Rancher's Perspective

BRENT ELDRIDGE

Necessary preservation of natural characteristics or unnecessary annihilation of culture and lifestyle? Essential elements in mineral- and forage-harvesting profit-hungry enterprises or exclusive high-country playgrounds of the rich and selfish? As wilderness-designation issues evolved over the last three decades, uncompromising preservation of pristine natural features ran head-on into uncompromising determination to save unfettered access to federal lands. Seldom has the debate been rational from either side, with commonplace misrepresentations and lack of concern for the other's values. It became an all-out war between those "selfish yuppies who would lock out all commercial uses and most visitors from the high country" and those "selfish entrepreneurs who rape and plunder in quest of profit." As a fourth-generation White Pine County rancher, I proudly joined the profit takers.

In spite of sentiments to the contrary, stockmen care for the land. Though it hasn't always been generally true, overgrazing today is not common. To overgraze repeatedly is to destroy the range, the very foundation of our livelihoods and lifestyles. Some advocacy groups' implications that the land needs designation to protect it from us have elicited justified anger and resentment among good rangeland ranchers throughout the West. Therefore, it should be understandable that stockmen have traditionally opposed locking up vast tracts of land that have heretofore been, for the most part, responsibly managed in a multiple-use fashion.

A somewhat stale preservationist argument relates to the "fact" that the Western cowboys' lifestyle is dying and "only a small percentage of the nation's food is raised on federal lands." It's almost as if that is the desired effect and exclusive special designation of large tracts are the means! You might imagine the frustration inherent in anticipation of the end of one's very economic existence. Roads used daily in caring for and managing livestock could be closed and obliterated by the stroke of a pen—because of potential road closures, our rangeland infrastructure might become run-down artifacts due to our inability to maintain it. Our way of life would, indeed, go the way of the horse-drawn carriage following designation of wilderness that would close roads by which we access our nation's rangelands.

My perception of wilderness matured when I was faced with the reality of impending designation of a large part of my family's summer range. After one of our summer ranges was included in the Nevada USFS Wilderness Bill, but prior to its passage, I met with wilderness advocates to negotiate a practical and enforceable boundary. My goal was to concede for designation all land which absolutely met legislative criteria but to exclude all existing roads essential to outdoor recreation, limited mineral exploration, and proper livestock management. During negotiations I was surprised to be met with sincere consideration of the logistics in managing commercial uses on federal lands, especially livestock grazing—with a little give and take, an agreement was reached. With the exception of our disagreement over several key roads on a neighboring allotment, our recommendation excluded all roads from designation; it was agreed that several recently pioneered trails be recommended for closure. Congress split the difference regarding the several key roads upon which we hadn't agreed; the large part of our agreement became the designation adopted in the bill and it was soon thereafter passed and signed into law. Except for a few corners cut in drawing the legislation map and the ostensible prohibition on administratively maintaining infrastructure with motorized equipment, we've experienced no adverse effects. Because our stock ponds now need maintenance, the currently asserted administrative exemption allowing motorized maintenance will be explored.

That designation, at least for the time being, has generally settled the issue of reasonable access to, and protection of, those particular federal lands. Now looms a new threat—indiscriminate four-wheeler use, which will ultimately put tire tracks on all the federal land in America if not adequately addressed. Since the relatively recent invasion by ATVs, roads have been pioneered into areas I've considered off-limits to vehicular travel, whether by my vehicle or someone else's. Unless steps are taken to prohibit the roading of back-country areas, that activity will destroy our ability to reasonably protect and enjoy those remote areas in the absence of motorized visitation. While I adamantly support and defend reasonable access to all federal lands, I also believe "reasonable access" means "no prohibition of travel which doesn't significantly and permanently damage resources." Because of severe erosion caused by extreme surface disturbance, our high, steep forests can't tolerate indiscriminate ATV use as generally can lower, gentler slopes and flats. It's an uncomfortable position for an anti-designation person like me to be in, advocating protection to meet this problem. Unfortunately, in my view, unless road pioneering is restricted by some more-palatable, less-exclusive means, wilderness designation may be the only adequate response.

Conversely, I'm torn between reasonable protection of our wilderness resources and unreasonable impacts upon our industrialized society as a whole. As ranchers ply their trade on both federal and private lands, they make use of hundreds of tools and conveniences that are the basic necessities for efficient food production. Proper livestock care and production employ the use of road vehicles, farm and construction equipment, windmills, powered pumps, generators, metal and plastic pipe, central-station electricity, appliances, electronics, liquid fuels, non-metallic minerals, and metal wire and posts, along with many other things. Without those products of mining remaining available at reasonable prices, modern ranching will cease. As mining is incrementally excluded from federal land, ranch necessities will become less available and more costly. Indeed, there isn't an individual, industry, or enterprise in modern America that won't ultimately be adversely impacted by the assault on mining of federal lands. We'll pay dearly should our nation's mineral needs become served largely by foreign production—mining restriction and its result, whether intended or not, are, unfortunately, the cornerstones of the wilderness premise.

If I had my druthers, several things would happen. Users of federal land would agree on areas worthy of protective consideration. There would be no designated wilderness areas, but all users would respect the land by treading lightly. Traditional users would confer and negotiate with wilderness advocates to establish reasonable restrictions that wouldn't deny the mineral industry access to areas of potential or known mineral deposits. And all private-property rights on federal lands would be respected and protected by our citizens and our government.

As most of those things will never occur, I support limited wilderness designation as the only realistic alternative. Only a small portion of eastern Nevada's federal lands has experienced vehicular degradation, but erosion and other resource damage is accelerating in those areas due to proliferating off-road vehicle use on steep or fragile slopes. I believe designation is the only measure capable of reversing the trend. Following designation, there should be, of course, steps taken by the federal government to compensate for any takings or other adverse impacts to property rights in the designated areas.

Splinter of the Moon—A Prayer for Nevada's Wild Places

ROBERTA MOORE

There is something very rich about the experience of being alone at the end of the day in the middle of wild country. Watching the sun lay its last blush of light on the land, mixing with the long shadows of coming nightfall, there is a hushed calm. I listen to the quiet doings of unseen creatures at the end of the day and feel a connection that brings me solace and comfort. It is here, in wild places, that I find my heart.

I remember many evenings when I lay silently in the sand, watching the day melt out of the sky and listening to the wilderness. In landscapes most people assume are empty, I would lie with an ear close to the earth, listening to the music of silence, broken by the dog song of coyotes. As light left the horizon and night would drape a shawl across the shoulders of mountains, I would sit, like an obedient child, waiting for the moon.

And as a small splinter of light rose in the blue-black velvet, I would watch the fragment of moon rise to just above the shadow of mountains and then, from deep within myself, I would begin my prayers—that I will live enough days in my life to see that small splinter of moon achieve fullness and that

I will live to see the small pieces of wilderness, sanctuaries for those of us who seek healing in wild places, brought to wholeness.

Our cities and communities have become frightening places in recent times. In Nevada, most of our state remains unaffected by the neon gaudiness. Basins rest between mountain ranges, and broad stretches of sagebrush climb to the fringe of pinyon-juniper woodlands and still higher to subalpine forests and mountain summits where snow sticks year-round.

In this unique landscape, as much as we are reminded of our valuable natural heritage, we are also reminded of the value of our cultural heritage—those Nevadans who live on the land. This is a land with a long history of human inhabitation, a place where settlers came to work the land and where people like me came because of wide open spaces. In Nevada, we hold our legacies, our various cultures, close to our hearts. In letting go of wilderness, we stand to let go of something much more—our identity.

Why wilderness designation? Why protect our natural resources? Because we need to protect ourselves. Granted, approximately 87 percent of Nevada is public land, but that label does not guarantee protection. Public land agencies aren't always adverse to development, and if development is allowed along the edges of sacred places and paths that lead to our personal sanctuaries, all too soon those cherished places will never be the same again, ever. Some will vanish completely.

In a busy, mechanized society, there is in each of us a place that prays for quiet. We yearn sometimes to get away from all the madness. We need those places—tree altars and sandy pews, rumbling creeks and dry riverbeds—where we can connect with something more real than neon facades.

One of my personal heroes, naturalist Sigurd Olson, recognized the perils of our expanding population and the decimation of the land. "Wilderness we can hold onto now," Olson proposed, "will become the final bastions of the spirit of man." These sanctuaries are the only hope for those of us who seek them. In the solitude of wilderness, we are able find refuge in a world gone haywire with modern contraptions.

We are like spoiled children caught up in a fast-food mentality—I want it my way, and I want it now. But the supposed joy of immediate results is not always the answer. It not only results in depletion of the land, but also in depletion of the human spirit.

I ask those of you who love your way of life, who cherish the wide open spaces and personal legacies that keep you close to the land, to say a prayer for wild places. Say a prayer for the splinter of the moon that rises in the east, in the hope that you may live long enough to see it become full. Say a prayer for wilderness in the hope that it, too, may achieve fullness.

Nevada Wilderness—What Good Is It?

DAVE FOREMAN

Nevada. To most, the name conjures glittering casinos, topless showgirls in impossible headdresses, and stars like Wayne Newton. There's another Nevada, though. This is the Nevada scorned by the high-speed traveler on Interstate 80, the desolate waste of sagebrush steppe and seemingly barren mountain ranges in the distance.

Beyond the bright lights of Las Vegas and Reno, off the four lanes of the interstate, away from the cathouse and the slot machine emporium, lies the real Nevada. The Great Basin. A land of basin and range after basin and range, caught between the Sierra Nevada range and Cascades and the Rocky Mountains. Empty valleys carpeted in sage with herds of pronghorn flashing the bright white of their rumps; valleys that stretch your eyes farther than you thought you could see. Valleys flowing like seas, breaking against the far mountains. Mountains rising up a mile or more to hidden glacier-gouged basins with tiny lakes glistening like turquoise in the dry air of this cold desert. Forests of aspen, mountain mahogany, or white fir cloaking the high basins, the rolling summits. And above all, the patriarchs, gnarled, weathered, and deeply wise from their millennial lives—bristlecone pines.

This vast, empty quarter, lost between the great dividing ranges, is one of the wildest and least-populated regions in the temperate Northern Hemisphere. And with good reason. This is a lean, hungry land, with little fat to make men rich. Tiny Vermont produces more pounds of beef than does huge Nevada. Assignment to Nevada for a forest ranger is exile to Siberia—there is no industrial forestry to practice. And so huge road-less areas unfold across the landscape—the wilderness we hope will endure forever. The wilderness we are working to protect so it will endure forever.

So, is Nevada empty? Barren? Desolate? Is all the action in the casinos? All the beauty in haughty showgirls? Are the sage-filled valleys and blue mountains out yonder good only for the sheepherder, the cowman, the trapper, the two-bit miner with a bulldozer?

Ask the mountain lion in the Grant Range. Ask the bighorn in the Sheep Range. The elk in the Schell Creek Range. The Lahontan cutthroat in a stream cutting down from Toiyabe Crest. The sage sparrow lost in the immensity of the Black Rock Desert. The golden eagle riding the thermals over the Clan Alpine Range.

Listen to the answer in the wind-murmur through the ancient limbs of the bristlecone.

They know.

Maps of Nevada Wilderness Areas

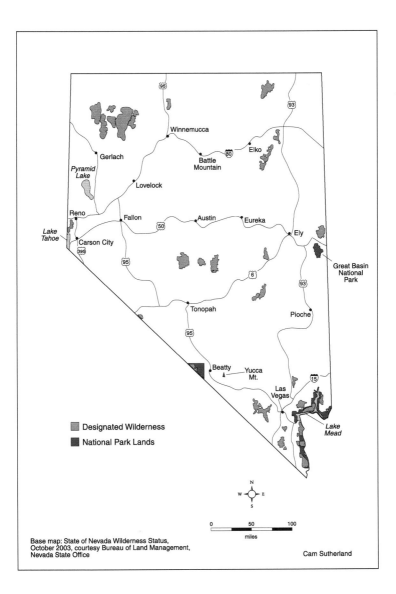

Gerlach

Winnemucca

Elko

Pyramid Lake

Battle Mountain

Lovelock

Reno   Fallon   Austin   Eureka

Lake Tahoe

Ely

Carson City

Great Basin National Park

Tonopah

Pioche

Beatty   Yucca Mt.

Las Vegas

Lake Mead

Designated Wilderness

National Park Lands

N
W E
S

0   50   100
miles

Base map: State of Nevada Wilderness Status, October 2003, courtesy Bureau of Land Management, Nevada State Office

Cam Sutherland

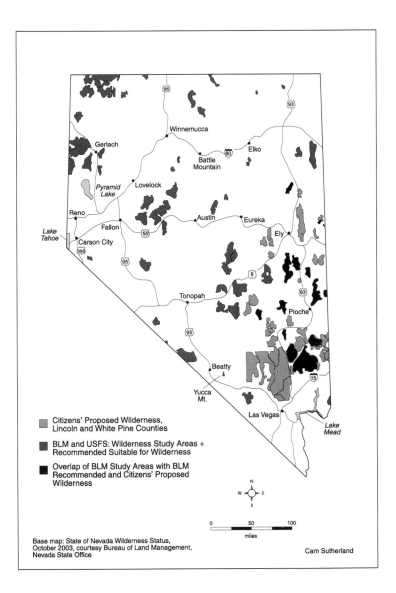

Citizens' Proposed Wilderness,
Lincoln and White Pine Counties

BLM and USFS: Wilderness Study Areas +
Recommended Suitable for Wilderness

Overlap of BLM Study Areas with BLM
Recommended and Citizens' Proposed
Wilderness

N
W   E
S

0   50   100
miles

Base map: State of Nevada Wilderness Status,
October 2003, courtesy Bureau of Land Management,
Nevada State Office

Cam Sutherland

Nevada's Protected Wild Places

Nevada wilderness designated in the Wilderness Act of 1964; signed into law on September 3, 1964.

Jarbidge Wilderness	64,667 acres USFS

Nevada wilderness designated in the Nevada Wilderness Protection Act of 1989; signed into law on December 5, 1989.

Alta Toquima Wilderness	38,000 acres USFS
Arc Dome Wilderness	115,000 acres USFS
Boundary Peak Wilderness	10,000 acres USFS
Currant Mountain Wilderness	36,000 acres USFS
East Humboldt Wilderness	36,900 acres USFS
Jarbidge Wilderness Additions	48,500 acres USFS
Mount Rose Wilderness	28,000 acres USFS
Quinn Canyon Wilderness	27,000 acres USFS
Ruby Mountain Wilderness	90,000 acres USFS
Mount Charleston Wilderness	43,000 acres USFS
Table Mountain Wilderness	98,000 acres USFS
Grant Range Wilderness	50,000 acres USFS
Mount Moriah Wilderness	82,000 acres USFS/BLM
Santa Rosa Wilderness	31,000 acres USFS

Nevada wilderness designated in the California Desert Protection Act of 1994; signed into law on October 31, 1994.

Death Valley National Park
  Nevada Triangle Wilderness   44,000 acres NPS

Nevada wilderness designated in the Black Rock Desert–High Rock Canyon Emigrant Trails National Conservation Area Act of 2000; signed into law on December 21, 2000.

Black Rock Desert Wilderness	315,700 acres BLM
Pahute Peak Wilderness	57,400 acres BLM
North Black Rock Range Wilderness	30,800 acres BLM
East Fork High Rock Canyon Wilderness	52,800 acres BLM
High Rock Lake Wilderness	59,300 acres BLM
Little High Rock Canyon Wilderness	48,700 acres BLM
High Rock Canyon Wilderness	46,600 acres BLM
Calico Mountains Wilderness	65,400 acres BLM
South Jackson Mountains Wilderness	56,800 acres BLM
North Jackson Mountains Wilderness	24,000 acres BLM

Nevada wilderness designated in Clark County Conservation of Public Land and Natural Resources Act of 2002; signed into law on November 6, 2002.

North McCullough Wilderness	14,763 acres BLM
South McCullough Wilderness	44,245 acres BLM

Wee Thump–Joshua Tree Wilderness	6,050 acres BLM
El Dorado Wilderness	31,950 acres NPS/BLM
Ireteba Peaks Wilderness	32,745 acres NPS/BLM
Jimbilnan Wilderness	18,879 acres NPS
Nellis Wash Wilderness	16,423 acres NPS
Spirit Mountain Wilderness	33,518 acres NPS/BLM
Arrow Canyon Wilderness	27,530 acres BLM
Bridge Canyon Wilderness	7,761 acres NPS
Black Canyon Wilderness	17,220 acres NPS/BLM
Pinto Valley Wilderness	39,173 acres NPS
Muddy Mountains Wilderness	48,019 acres BLM/NPS
Rainbow Mountain Wilderness	24,997 acres USFS/BLM
Lime Canyon Wilderness	23,233 acres BLM
Jumbo Springs Wilderness	4,631 acres BLM
Mt. Charleston Additions	13,598 acres USFS/BLM
La Madre Mountain Wilderness	47,180 acres USFS/BLM

Total acres of wilderness in Nevada: 2,016,490

CONTRIBUTORS

BRIAN BEFFORT, a fourth-generation Nevadan, is the Conservation Director for Friends of Nevada Wilderness. Before joining
Friends in 2001, he was the Outdoors Editor for the *Reno Gazette-
Journal.* He has a master's degree in journalism from the University
of Missouri, Columbia, and a bachelor's degree in anthropology
from Reed College.

PETER BRADLEY is a native Nevadan, born in Pioche. A natural-
ist and avid walker, he has traversed 3,900 miles in Nevada, New
Mexico, California, Oregon, and Washington. He holds a B.S. in
Wildlife Management and an M.S. in Ecology from the University of
Nevada, Reno.

RICHARD BRYAN, a Nevada native, served as Nevada's twenty-
sixth governor. Elected to the United States Senate in 1988, Bryan has
committed himself to keeping nuclear waste out of Nevada. He was
instrumental in the designation of the Black Rock Conservation
Area, and his public record speaks highly of his commitment to his
home state.

JON CHRISTENSEN is the author of *Nevada,* a book of essays
celebrating the Silver State with photos by Deon Reynolds. He is a
former Knight Journalism Fellow at Stanford University and Stein-

beck Fellow at San Jose State University. Christensen has written for many of Nevada's newspapers, as well as *The New York Times, High Country News,* and other newspapers and magazines. He produced the Nevada Public Radio series "Nevada Variations," an audio portrait of each of the state's seventeen counties. And he is editor-at-large for *GreatBasinNews.com* and *ConservationNews.org.* Although he has returned to California for an extended sojourn, home still means Nevada.

MICHAEL P. COHEN taught in the English Department at the University of Southern Utah for twenty-seven years. At present he teaches at the University of Nevada, Reno. His book *The Pathless Way: John Muir and American Wilderness* won the Mark H. Ingraham Prize at the University of Wisconsin Press. *The History of the Sierra Club, 1872–1970* was published in 1988, and *A Garden of Bristlecones: Tales of Change in the Great Basin* appeared in 1998.

BRENT ELDRIDGE, a native of White Pine County, Nevada, is a rancher who has committed himself to the preservation and restoration of his native state. He has served on various advisory boards for the BLM, is a past director of the Nevada Cattlemen's Association, and is a past chairman of the Nevada Land Action Association. Eldridge served as a White Pine County Commissioner for twelve years and currently serves on the Bureau of Land Management National Wild Horse Advisory Board and the Eastern Nevada Landscape Coalition Board of Trustees.

DAVE FOREMAN is one of America's best-known conservation leaders. He has worked as a Washington, D.C., lobbyist for the Wilderness Society, served on the Sierra Club Board of Directors, and co-founded *Wild Earth Journal* and the Wildlands Project, for which he served as publisher and chairman, respectively. He is the author of a novel, *The Lobo Outback Funeral Home,* and two works of nonfiction, *The Big Outside* (with Howie Wolke) and *Confessions of an Eco-Warrior.*

MICHAEL FROME is a well-known author, educator, and activist. His books include *Greenspeak—Fifty Years of Environmental Muckraking and Advocacy, Green Ink—An Introduction to Environmental Journalism,* and *Battle for the Wilderness.* He lives in Port Washington, Wisconsin.

CHERYLL GLOTFELTY became the nation's first professor of Literature and Environment when she joined the faculty at the University of Nevada, Reno, in 1990. She has since helped create the university's Graduate Program in Literature and Environment. In 1992 she co-founded the Association for the Study of Literature and Environment, an international organization of scholars and writers. She co-edited with Harold Fromm *The Ecocriticism Reader: Landmarks in Literary Ecology* and is currently editing a Nevada literary anthology.

SHAUN GRIFFIN is the founding director of the Community Chest, a non-profit agency serving children and families in northwestern Nevada, and former founding director of the state's homeless education office. For the past fourteen years he has volunteered at Northern Nevada Correctional Center to teach a poetry workshop. His latest book of poems is *Bathing in the River of Ashes,* published by the University of Nevada Press in 1999.

LILACE MELLIN GUIGNARD currently lives in Reno, where she teaches, writes poetry and essays, camps, hikes, and climbs. She was an environmental educator and activist in North Carolina before making a home in the Great Basin. This arid land has taught her new definitions of beauty.

CORBIN HARNEY is a Western Shoshone elder and spiritual leader from Newe Segobia (The People's Land). Harney has not had any college education, yet he speaks eloquently to students, government officials, and members of the public about the dire situation of our environment, especially because of radiation damage from nuclear testing, storage, and transportation on our roads and railways. He lives in Tecopa, California.

LINDA HUSSA is a poet, essayist, and rancher living in Cedarville, California. Her books include *Diary of a Cow Camp Cook; Where the Wind Lives; Ride the Silence; Lige Langston: Sweet Iron;* and *Blood Sister, I Am to These Fields.*

COREY LEE LEWIS moved to Nevada from Kansas five years ago to pursue his doctorate in Literature and Environment at the University of Nevada, Reno. He completed his Ph.D. in 2003 with a dissertation titled "Reading the Trail: Exploring the Literature and Natural History of the California Crest." He teaches in the English

Department at the University of Nevada, supervises field crews for the Nevada Conservation Corps, and serves on the advisory board of Friends of Nevada Wilderness.

ROBERT MCGINTY is a fourth-generation Nevadan. He spends his free time hiking, hunting, fishing, and horseback riding in the wild areas of the northeastern part of the state. He and his wife Celia have two children and have lived in Elko, Nevada, for the past twenty-five years.

REBECCA MILLS, former superintendent of Nevada's Great Basin National Park, has had a long history of public service. Retired and now residing in California to be near her family, Becky and her partner Dave Sharp (a Nevadan from Ruby Valley) have a small trailer home in Baker, Nevada. They return often to explore Nevada's wild places and volunteer with Great Basin National Park, the Nature Conservancy, and other conservation groups.

ROBERTA MOORE resides in Baker, Nevada, with her husband David, in a 400-acre bird and wildlife sanctuary that the Moore family donated to the Nevada Land Conservancy in December 1999. She presently works for Great Basin National Park as a park ranger. As an artist and writer, she focuses on the preservation and restoration of Nevada's wild and beautiful landscapes.

STEVEN NIGHTINGALE, a longtime Reno resident, is the author of two novels, *The Lost Coast* and *The Thirteenth Daughter of the Moon.* He currently lives in Spain.

K. ALDEN PETERSON has supported Nevada wilderness efforts for more than twenty years. Working in the fields of photography, film making, painting, and creative fiction and nonfiction writing, Peterson strives to pierce the veil of culture drawn between humans and the earth. Currently he resides in Reno, where he is studying environmental sustainability as a student at the University of Nevada.

LAURA RAINEY-CARPENTER, a registered member of the Ely Shoshone Tribe, has had an extensive career as an engineer, working for the Clark County Planning Department, private engineers, and Newport News Shipbuilding (where she worked on the coolant piping system of the aircraft carrier *Nimitz*); she completed her career as Senior Electrical Designer for Raytheon Services of Nevada at the Nevada Test Site. She is also a silversmith and now operates Smoke Signals Trading Post in Ely. She is working to establish a Native American Cultural Center for Great Basin tribes in order to preserve their heritage.

HARRY REID was born in Searchlight, Nevada, and has distinguished himself as a defender of Nevada's rights. Elected to the United States Senate in 1986, Reid has assembled an impressive legislative and leadership record for the people of Nevada. His published record speaks for itself.

ROBERT LEONARD REID is the author of two books, *America, New Mexico* and the mountaineering memoir *Mountains of the Great Blue Dream,* and editor of the anthology *A Treasury of the Sierra Nevada.* He is director of contemporary music at St. Peter's Episcopal

Church in Carson City and the keyboard player in the oldies band Lost at the Lake.

ANN RONALD, Foundation Professor of English at the University of Nevada, Reno, is the author of *GhostWest: Reflections Past and Present, Earthtones: A Nevada Album* (with photographs by Stephen Trimble), *The New West of Edward Abbey,* and *Reader of the Purple Sage: Essays on Western Writers and Environmental Literature.*

GARY SHORT has been a Stegner Fellow at Stanford University and a fellow at the Fine Arts Work Center in Provincetown, Massachusetts. His second collection of poems, *Flying Over Sonny Liston,* received the Western States Book Award. He has been a professor at the University of Alaska, Fairbanks, and Old Dominion University. He currently divides his time between Virginia City and Guatemala.

MARGE SILL has been an advocate for wilderness for more than fifty years. She worked for the passage of the 1964 Wilderness Act, the 1984 California Wilderness Act, the 1989 Nevada Wilderness Legislation, and the passage of wilderness legislation in northern Nevada and Clark County in 2000 and 2002. She was also active in the establishment of Great Basin National Park. Known as the "Mother of Nevada Wilderness," her focus as a writer, until now, has been poetry.

SCOTT SLOVIC is professor of Literature and Environment at the University of Nevada, Reno. From 1995 to 2002, he directed UNR's Center for Environmental Arts and Humanities, and he currently chairs the English Department's graduate program in Literature and Environment. From 1992 to 1995, he served as founding president of the Association for the Study of Literature and Environment. He is the author, editor, or co-editor of eleven books, including the recent anthologies *Getting Over the Color Green: Contemporary Environmental Literature of the Southwest*, *The ISLE Reader: Ecocriticism, 1993–2003*, and *What's Nature Worth? Narrative Expressions of Environmental Values*. He edits the scholarly journal *ISLE: Interdisciplinary Studies in Literature and Environment* and two book series: Milkweed Editions' Credo Series and the University of Nevada Press's Environmental Arts and Humanities Series.

GARY SNYDER is a poet, essayist, activist, and forest-dweller on the western slope of the Sierra in the Yuba River drainage. He crosses the pass and travels the Great Basin whenever he can. His most recent book of poetry is *Mountains and Rivers Without End*.

PATRICIA SWAIN spent much of her childhood in New York State on 160 wooded acres that included a lake, turtles, and muskrats. She held various editorial positions in New York City: Crowell-Collier, Funk & Wagnalls, a few small magazines. She then joined the staff of a freewheeling Coconut Grove, Florida, biweekly called *The Village Post*. She won a "Gutsy" award for her writing in that publication. She then migrated west and taught Freshman English at the University of Nevada, Reno, and Developmental English at Truckee Meadows Community College. She is currently editing the little wrinkled notebooks that have ridden in her backpack for thirty years of walking meditations.

STEPHEN TRIMBLE has published eighteen books, including *The Geography of Childhood: Why Children Need Wild Places* (with Gary Nabhan) and *The People: Indians of the American Southwest.* Trimble's fieldwork in Nevada wildlands spans more than twenty years and has led to *The Sagebrush Ocean: A Natural History of the Great Basin,* winner of The Sierra Club's Ansel Adams Award for photography and conservation and of The High Desert Museum's Chiles Award, and *Earthtones: A Nevada Album* (with essays by Ann Ronald), winner of the Wilbur S. Shepperson Humanities Book Award. Trimble co-compiled (with Terry Tempest Williams) the landmark collection by writers hoping to sway public policy: *Testimony: Writers of the West Speak on Behalf of Utah Wilderness.* Trimble lives in Salt Lake City.

TERRY TEMPEST WILLIAMS is a lifelong resident of the Great Basin and currently lives in Castle Valley, Utah. Her many awards include a Lannan Literary Fellowship and a Guggenheim Fellowship, and her books include *Refuge, Leap,* and, most recently, *Red: Passion and Patience in the Desert.*

ANN ZWINGER received the John Burroughs Medal for *Run, River, Run* and the Western States Book Award for *Downcanyon.* The author of many books exploring the natural history of the American West, Zwinger lives in Colorado Springs, Colorado.